POCKET
REFERENCE

for
Writers

POCKET REFERENCE

for

Writers

THIRD EDITION

Toby Fulwiler
University of Vermont

■

Alan R. Hayakawa
The Patriot News
Harrisburg, Pennsylvania

PEARSON
Prentice Hall

Upper Saddle River, New Jersey 07458

Library of Congress Cataloging-in-Publication Data

Fulwiler, Toby
   Pocket reference for writers / Toby Fulwiler and Alan R. Hayakawa.—3rd ed.
     p. cm.
   Includes index.
   ISBN 0-13-614237-0
   1. English language—Rhetoric—Handbooks, manuals, etc.   2. English language—
Grammar—Handbooks, manuals, etc.   3. Report writing—Handbooks, manuals, etc.
I. Hayakawa, Alan R.   II. Title
   PE1408.F815 2008
   808'.042—dc22

                                                                        20007006266

Editorial Director: Leah Jewell
Editor in Chief: Craig Campanella
Executive Editor: Kevin Molloy
Project Manager: Melissa Casciano
Editorial Assistant: Megan Dubrowskl
VP/Director, Production and Manufacturing: Barbara Kittle
Director, Marketing: Brandy Dawson
Senior Marketing Manager: Windley Morley
Marketing Assistant: Kimberly Caldwell
Copyeditor: Laura Patchkofsky
Manufacturing Manager: Nick Sklitsis
Assistant Manufacturing Manager: Mary Ann Gloriande
Creative Design Director: Leslie Osher
Art Director, Interior and Cover Design:
     Laura Gardner/Running River Design
Image Resource Center Director: Melinda Patelli
Rights and Permissions Manager: Zina Arabia
Visual Research Manager: Beth Brenzel
Image Permissions Coordinator: Ang'john Ferreri
Cover Visual Research and Permissions Manager: Karen Sanatar
Cover Image Coordinator: Rita Wenning
Cover Image: Royalty Free/Corbis
Full-Service Project Management: Karen Berry/Pine Tree Composition, Inc.
Composition: Pine Tree Composition, Inc.
Printer/Binder: RR Donnelley & Sons
Cover Printer: Coral Graphics

Pearson Education LTD.
Pearson Education Singapore, Pte. Ltd
Pearson Education, Canada, Ltd
Pearson Education–Japan
Pearson Education Australia PTY, Limited
Pearson Education North Asia Ltd
Pearson Educación de Mexico, S.A. de C.V.
Pearson Education Malaysia, Pte. Ltd
Pearson Education, Upper Saddle River, New Jersey

10 9 8 7 6 5 4 3 2 1
ISBN-13: 978-0-13-614237-9
ISBN-10:   0-13-614237-0

PART one
Writing in College

Every act of writing addresses three questions: (1) Why are you writing? (2) Who is your audience? and (3) What is your situation? How you answer these questions largely shapes the voice you project on paper. To help you figure out the **Purpose, Audience, Situation,** and **Voice** in any writing task, it helps to have a reliable **Writing Process** that works for you. Part I concludes with a chapter focused on the essential skill of **Reading Images Critically.**

1   *Writing with Purpose*

When you write a personal letter, you know why you are doing it and what you hope to accomplish. However, when you write in response to a school assignment, your instructor sets the purpose, and it becomes your job to figure it out. Regardless of who instigates it, thoughtful writing is purposeful writing. To succeed, you need to know why you are writing and what you hope to accomplish.

1 a Writing to discover

Writing helps people think as well as record what they've already thought. Writing makes language, and therefore thought, visible and permanent, allowing writers to understand, critique, rearrange, and correct their ideas. Discovery writing is written primarily for the writer, not for a distant or judgmental audience. Consequently, style, structure, and correctness matter less in discovery writing than invention, exploration, and honesty. Forms of discovery writing include the following:

- Freewriting
- Journal and diary writing
- Letters or e-mail to trusted people
- Personal notes and lists
- Early drafts of formal papers

Although instructors sometimes ask to see samples of discovery writing, they seldom correct or evaluate it. Whether assigned or not, such informal writing will help you learn virtually any subject better. You are writing to discover when you think about how to approach assignments, find topics, locate research sources, or just find out what's on your mind. (For more on discovery writing, see Chapters 7–11.)

1 b Writing to communicate

The general purpose of most writing in college and the world at large is to communicate to audiences other than the writer. More specific purposes include communicating with the intention of reporting, informing, persuading, and exploring. To communicate clearly, writing needs to be

- clear, to be understood;
- conventional, to enhance understanding and minimize confusion; and
- supported and documented, to create belief or bolster credibility.

You are writing to communicate when an assignment asks you to *explain, report, analyze, describe, discuss, compare, contrast, interpret, argue,* or *evaluate* to an audience other than yourself. The majority of this pocket handbook explains and illustrates the conventions and guidelines most appropriate for academic writing. (For more information on academic writing, see Part Three.)

1 c Writing to create

Creative writers pay special attention to form, shape, rhythm, imagery, and the symbolic qualities of language. The term *creative writing* is usually associated with poetry, fiction, and drama but should apply to any text written with care, craft, and originality. For example, researching slave conditions in 1850s Virginia and then writing a narrative from the point of view of an escaped slave can be a creative yet highly factual paper at the same time—interesting to write and interesting to read. Although creative writing is also a type of communicative writing, its focus is less on audience and more on the shape of the expression itself.

Only a few college assignments may ask you to write explicitly creative papers, but many more conventional papers will profit from imaginative approaches that increase reader interest. You are invited to write creatively when an assignment asks you to *suppose, speculate, design, imagine, create,* or *invent.*

2 | *Addressing an Audience*

Writing is successful when it communicates clearly to its intended audience. To address readers effectively, it helps if you imagine what they already know and believe as well as what their questions might be. Note how differently you would write to a friend than a college instructor. With your friend, you assume shared experiences and a common sense of humor, allowing you to be playful with both content and style. With your instructor, however, you can assume very little, which means you need to explain a lot—and very carefully.

Instructors are especially difficult audiences because (1) they know what they expect from their assignment, (2) they often know more about the subject of your paper than you do, and (3) each has a personally distinct set of expectations. However, all instructors expect papers to demonstrate *accurate knowledge, critical reasoning,* and *literate language skills.*

- **Knowledge.** A successful paper demonstrates what you know and how well you know it. If you argue for or against affirmative action policies, for example, you must demonstrate that you know about recent civil rights history and current political debates. A successful college paper has accurate facts, clear definitions, careful explanations, up-to-date information, and correct documentation for ideas borrowed from other sources.

- **Critical reasoning.** A successful paper reveals your ability to reason logically and consistently, to evaluate ideas and arguments, to support assertions, to organize information, and to be persuasive. In arguing for or against tighter gun control laws, offer good reasons for your position and refute opposing arguments. Critical reasoning is witnessed in the clarity and arrangement of your ideas, the justness of your claims, and the persuasiveness of your evidence.

- **Language skills.** Instructors notice the clarity and correctness of your language, especially when your sentences are not clear or your spelling, punctuation, or grammar is incorrect. You are expected to turn in papers that are neat, legible, and carefully edited according to standard academic conventions (see Parts Nine through Twelve).

3 | *Assessing the Situation*

When you write college papers, remember that you are in an academic community that may differ in important ways from a home, high school, or work community. The academic community has clear expectations for what acceptable papers should do and how they should appear. Instructors, regardless of discipline, look for the following elements in academic writing:

- **Truth.** Regardless of department or discipline, members of the university community are committed to the pursuit of truth. Each academic discipline pursues truth in a particular way—the sciences rely on a rigorous scientific method; the social sciences quantify whatever can be counted; the humanities emphasize individual perceptions. A successful college paper uses the knowledge and methods of the discipline in which it has been assigned to pursue something as accurate, believable, and true as possible—all the while recognizing that capturing something that is absolutely true is difficult if not impossible.

- **Evidence.** Scholars in all disciplines use credible evidence to support the truths they claim. Scientists make claims about the physical and biological world and cite evidence to support those claims; political scientists make claims about political processes, people, and institutions; art historians make claims about creative expression, and so on. As a college writer, make claims, assertions, or arguments you believe to be true; then support those with the best facts, examples, and illustrations available. Always document the sources for this evidence.

- **Balance.** It is difficult or even impossible to prove that something is absolutely true because new information constantly calls old conclusions into question. Consequently, academic writers make claims cautiously, using balanced, judicious language positioned somewhere between authority and doubt. Your own authority as a college writer will be based on how well you read, reason, and write. Academic convention suggests that you present your inferences, assertions, and arguments in neutral, serious, nonemotional language and be fair to opposing points of view.

4 Finding Your Voice

Writing voices range from assertive to tentative, loud to quiet, serious to sarcastic, clear to garbled, and so on. Each of us is capable of projecting one or more of these voices at one time or another. Some voices win people over and inspire trust whereas others do not, so you need to figure out how best to project your own voice in a variety of situations. An appropriate voice for a particular paper reflects the larger academic community in which you are writing as well as your own unique background and personal experience. Your purpose, audience, and situation go a long way toward determining that voice—and so does who you are and where you come from. Think about the *tone, style, structure,* and *bias* of the voice you present in your writing.

■ **Tone.** The attitude you adopt toward a subject and audience is reflected in your tone: passionate, indifferent, puzzled, friendly, annoyed, and so on. Tone is something you control in everyday speech when you speak gently to a baby, cautiously to a teacher, or sarcastically to your friends. On paper, you control tone by selecting and emphasizing words, sentence type, and punctuation to approximate the mood you want to project. To control tone, read out loud everything you write and ask yourself, Does it sound as I intend? If not, rewrite until it does.

■ **Style.** Style includes your choice and use of words, the construction and length of sentences, and the way the grammar and mechanics present your ideas on the page. Style can be described as formal (careful in respect to both convention and assertion), informal (more casual in form and mechanics), or colloquial (which sounds like talk written down). Unless circumstances dictate otherwise, write college papers in a semiformal style that is clear, precise, and direct yet sounds like a real human being speaking—perhaps a style similar to that used in this handbook.

■ **Structure.** Structure concerns the organization of a whole paper and the relationships among the parts within the paper. The structure of a text suggests the thought process that created it. For example, writing with a logical structure suggests similar habits of mind, whereas writing with a circular or associative structure suggests more intuitive habits of mind. Some papers might call for a more logical self, others a more intuitive self; skillful writers could go either way. To control structure ask yourself, How should the text open? Where should it go next? How should it conclude?

■ **Bias.** When you write, you convey—directly or indirectly—what you believe socially, politically, culturally, and so on. Unless you deliberately mislead, your personal biases will be somewhere in the foreground or background of everything you write. Learn when personal values are expected (personal essays) and when they are not (lab reports). Examine drafts for opinion and judgment words that reveal your values, and keep or remove these words as appropriate.

5 | Strategic Writing

Some strategies work better than others to produce good writing. At the same time, a particular strategy that works for one writer may not work for another. This chapter explains some basic approaches to successful writing and asks you to practice the approach that works best for you.

Good papers sometimes begin as vague notions, other times as specific intentions, so approaches to particular papers vary even for an individual writer. At the same time, for the vast majority of writers, some elements of composing remain constant. For example, no matter how a paper begins or how good a first draft may be, rewriting nearly always makes it better. And important papers conclude with careful editing and line–by–line proofreading to guarantee clarity, accuracy, and correctness. Despite these elements common to most successful writing, there is no formula to follow that guarantees success. So, despite variations in purpose, audience, circumstance, and skill, we believe most writers will profit from a close examination of the several phases of writing we might call the "writing process."

For discussion purposes, look at five distinct phases of writing in the approximate order in which they might occur in most writing tasks: *planning, drafting, researching, revising,* and *editing*—although they may occur in any order, at different times, and more than once as you write. Regardless of how you actually use these phases, what matters is that you understand how each one, carefully practiced, leads to successful papers.

- **Planning.** Asking questions, trying out answers, and developing and discarding directions are all part of getting started. You are planning deliberately when you make notes, turn casual lists into organized outlines, write journal entries, compose rough drafts, and consult with others. You also plan less deliberately while you walk, jog, eat, read, and converse with friends or when you wake up in the middle of the night with an idea. Planning occurs, one way or another, every time you think about something you need to write. (See Chapters 7–11 for specific planning strategies.)

- **Drafting.** At some point, all writers move beyond planning and actually start writing. Drafting happens when you try to advance your solution to a problem and see whether or not it works. The secret to productive writing is sitting down and beginning. A first draft is concerned with developing ideas, finding direction, clarifying concepts—in short, finding out what, exactly, the paper needs to say. Of course, you hope that your first draft will be final, but a rereading often suggests otherwise. (See Chapters 12–14 for drafting strategies.)

- **Researching.** College papers require precise information rather than vague knowledge. For such papers, active researching may take place prior to any drafting or while the writing is going on. The library and Internet provide new textual information, while interviews and site visits supply field data. Research also includes

rereading textbooks, consulting dictionaries, conducting laboratory experiments, asking questions, and visiting museums. (See Chapters 17–23 for in-depth
strategies for writing with research.)

■ **Revising.** Somewhere in the middle to later stages of
composing, writers begin revising the drafts they have
planned, drafted, and researched. Revising involves
rewriting to make the purpose clearer, the argument
stronger, the details sharper, the evidence more convincing, the organization more logical. True revising is
not just tinkering with words and punctuation but re-
seeing ideas and thinking again about direction, arguments, and evidence. (See Chapters 15–16 for revision
strategies.)

■ **Editing.** Editing means sharpening, condensing, and
clarifying the language. Editing is paying careful attention to specific words, striving for the most clarity and
punch possible. Editing is rearranging sentences, finding strong verbs, and eliminating wordy constructions.
The final stage of editing is proofreading—reading line
by line with a ruler, correcting errors in spelling, typos,
punctuation, and grammar. (See Chapters 43–66 for
editing strategies.)

6 | *Reading Images Critically*

To critically understand contemporary texts, readers and
writers need to understand visual as well as verbal
language. This chapter examines the basic elements of
visual communication and raises questions useful to both
critical reader and writer.

6 a   The elements of composition

To compose either an effective essay or a strong picture, com-
posers in both visual and verbal media present **information**
from a composer's **point of view.** Each also creates meaningful **themes** through careful **arrangement**—pictures in
two-dimensional space, stories in sequential time.

How many words would it take?

Information

In English, information is conveyed in words written sequentially, left to right, directing readers' attention toward meaning. However, in visual images, information is presented simultaneously so viewers start or stop anywhere they like.

In the accompanying photograph, "Roadside Stand," by Walker Evans, what do you see first? The informality of the roadside market in contrast with today's modern supermarkets? The careful order in an otherwise low-rent store? The two boys holding the watermelons? The verbal signs that advertise "Honest Weights, Square Dealings"? Is the sign reassuring or suspicious? And if the photo supports the cliché, "a picture is worth a thousand words," with which words would you begin to explain the meaning of this photo?

To think critically about visual *information,* first identify what objects, facts, processes, or symbols are portrayed in the image. Taking all the information together, ask if there is a main or unifying idea: Is the meaning open to multiple interpretations? Is it suggested, but not stated? Or is it clear and unambiguous?

Point of View

In written texts, *point of view* refers to the "person" from whose vantage point the information is delivered. In photographs, drawings, or paintings, *point of view* refers

How does point of view shape this picture?

to the place from which the image-maker looks at the subject—where the photographer places his camera, the artist her easel. A camera aimed east omits information north, west, and south, and so on.

In the photograph of the Filipino lettuce pickers by Dorothea Lange, what first catches your attention—the dirt gullies, the big lettuces, the open sky, or the stooped figures? If the people, what is noteworthy about them—size? clothing? arrangement? Where has Lange placed her camera? How does her camera placement affect the meaning you attach to the photo?

To think critically about *point of view,* ask where is the viewer standing? How does the view shape how the audience thinks or feels about the subject? What would happen if the vantage point were higher, lower, or somewhere else?

Arrangement and Pattern

The term *arrangement* in visual texts is similar to terms such as *order, organization,* and *structure* in verbal texts. While writers put together a story, essay, or poem to take place over the time it takes a reader to follow the text, line by line, photographers arrange two-dimensional images to make meaning in space rather than time. In visual texts, then, *arrangement* refers to the ways the various parts of a picture come together, one way or another, and how they lead the viewer's eye toward meaning.

In Dorothea Lange's photo of the plowed field (page 12), how does the curving pattern of the furrowed field lines contribute to the meaning of this photograph? How do the

How does pattern shape meaning?

patterns of light and dark also contribute? And what is the role of the single human dwelling in this carefully plowed plain? Does it help to know that Lange's photo is dated 1938?

To think critically about *arrangement,* ask: Where is the center of gravity? Was it found or fabricated? Where do patterns of light/dark, large/small, and number lead the eye? What does the arrangement suggest about the meaning of the image?

Theme

Both verbal and visual texts may be said to have themes—statements that identify the larger meaning of the text. In verbal texts, theme may be stated. In a visual text, theme must be inferred by the viewer.

Which is more important, words or image?

In Marian Post Wolcott's photo of a Depression–era movie theater, what visual elements first catch your attention? The man ascending the angled staircase? The graphic and stark light and dark patterns? And what do the signs contribute to this particular image? Does the fine print help? Would the Wolcott photo mean the same if either verbal language or photographic image were subtracted?

To think critically about *theme,* ask what catches your attention first? Second? What emotions do you feel and why? How do the elements of *information, point of view,* and *arrangement* combine to create theme?

6 b Color

In verbal texts, the word "color" is metaphorical and commonly refers to rich details that flesh out a description. In visual texts, color shows us the full range of colors we see with our eyes.

Look, for instance, at the photo of New York City firefighters raising an American flag at Ground Zero. The original is in color, but we added a black and white version for comparison. What is your reaction to seeing the two versions side by side? Which is more powerful? Why? What do the colors signify? Red, white, and blue? Gray, white, or black? Are these meanings arbitrary or logical?

To think critically about color, notice whether it enhances or distorts the reality of the image. What would be lost, what gained if color were subtracted?

Both words and pictures in the hands of skilled writers, artists, and photographers can be powerfully persuasive. Consequently, both verbal language and visual images need to be viewed critically to understand, first, the meaning of the message and, second, the intent behind the meaning. As writers and creators of images, the same critical understanding will advance your own writing and art.

WRITING ACROSS THE CURRICULUM

Photographs as Disciplinary Documents

Choose any single image in this chapter, and write a page or two, reimagining it through the eyes of a specific academic discipline:

- Imagine it as a document from which to infer **historical** change. Where would you go to take a contemporary photo with similar subject matter?

- Imagine it as an **economic** or **sociological** document. What details would you highlight? With what specific socioeconomic group would you compare them today?

- Imagine it as a **poem** or **short story.** What verbal image would begin your poem? What character name would begin your story?

- Imagine the photo used in a **political** or **religious campaign:** who would use it and what purpose would the photo serve in the campaign?

- Imagine the photo as a **work of art.** What is aesthetically strong and not dated? What contemporary photographer or aesthetic movement might this work have influenced?

- Imagine the photo as part of a poster for a current **advocacy group.** Which group? What would the poster say?

- Imagine the photo as an **advertisement.** Name the product. How would you pitch it?

PART two
Writing to Discover

For many writers, the most difficult part of writing is getting started. It is especially daunting to write a paper that will be evaluated for a grade, so it is easy to put off the writing until the night before it is due. However, trying to write both the first and the final draft at the last minute seldom results in either good learning or good writing. The chapters in this section will help start any paper in a more thoughtful manner.

7 | *Freewriting to Find Ideas*

Freewriting is writing quickly without worrying about rules. To freewrite, deliberately write as fast as possible and free-associate, allowing one word to trigger the next and one idea to lead to another. Ideas happen when you write intensely, nonstop, and without censoring, drawing thoughts from wherever in your mind they may reside. If you haven't freewritten before, the following suggestions will help.

- Write fast for a fixed period of time, say, ten minutes, on whatever problem needs solving or topic needs finding.

- Write the whole ten minutes without stopping to check spelling or word choice, stare at the ceiling, or think. So long as you continue writing, the words will generate the thoughts.

- Write to yourself. Don't worry about digressing or writing something silly. If you catch a new thought while writing even silly things, the freewriting has done its job.

To focus this technique, try a sequence of freewrites, each one starting with the most interesting sentence in the last freewrite, then looping back in on itself to push your idea ever deeper.

- Freewrite for ten minutes on a possible paper topic.

- Review your freewrite. Select one sentence, copy it to a fresh sheet of paper, and freewrite for another ten minutes.

- Repeat as often as necessary to locate your topic.

8 | *Journal Writing to Explore Ideas*

Journals are personal notebooks that allow writers to explore their own thoughts and feelings about anything that matters. Instructors commonly ask you to keep a journal to help you focus on the subject matter of a single discipline but also to speculate broadly on the whole range of your academic experience. A journal differs from other academic assignments in that it is written primarily for yourself, not the professor. Like diaries, journals are written in the first person ("I") about ideas related to a college subject that are important to the writer. Here are some guidelines for writing a successful journal:

- Date each entry.
- Use your natural voice (as in freewriting).
- Write regularly (several times a week if not daily).

Above all, journals are discovery and practice books in which you are free to try out new ideas. A well-kept journal will be the best possible record of your educational experience. The following suggestions will make journal writing useful in any college class:

- Explore potential topics, try sample introductions, make possible arguments, record relevant research, assess progress, and make plans for what to do next.
- Ask questions as you write: What's my point? What's missing? How might my argument be made stronger?
- Use a loose-leaf notebook so you can share relevant entries with your instructor while continuing to write in it for yourself.
- Look for connections between academic and personal knowledge.
- Respond informally to assigned readings to help you remember them better. What was the author's point? What interested me most?

WRITING ACROSS THE CURRICULUM

Characteristics of Darwin's Journal

Many scientists, philosophers, and writers have kept journals to both find ideas and create a record of those ideas to return to at a later date. The following excerpt is typed from the handwritten journal Charles Darwin kept aboard the *Beagle* in 1836 as he sailed around the Galapagos Islands off the coast of Ecuador, speculating about the workings of nature and generating ideas for what would later become the theory of evolution in *The Origin of Species* (1859). Describe the characteristics of Darwin's journal entry that identify it as writing aimed solely at himself and not a wider public audience. Can you see the value in such on-the-spot speculations written down and dated?

> *In the endless cycle of revolutions, by actions of rivers currents. & sea beaches. All mineral masses must have a tendency to mingle; The sea would separate quartzose sand from the finer matter resulting from degradation of Felspar & other minerals containing Alumen.—This matter accumulating in deep seas forms slates: How is the Lime separated; is it washed from the solid rock by the actions of Springs or more probably by some unknown Volcanic process? How does it come that all Lime is not accumulated in the Tropical oceans detained by Organic powers. We know the waters of the ocean all are mingled. These reflections might be introduced either in note in Coral Paper or hypothetical origin of some sandstones, as in Australia.—Have Limestones all been dissolved. if so sea would separate them from indissoluble rocks? Has Chalk ever been dissolved?*
>
> [*The Red Notebook of Charles Darwin.* Ed. S. Herbert.
> Cornell U. Press, 1980, pp. 37–38.]

9 | Clustering to See Ideas

Clustering is a method of listing ideas in a nonlinear way to reveal the relationships among them. Clustering is useful for both discovering and exploring a topic after you have done preliminary research. Like outlining, the act of clustering helps you invent and organize at the same time. To create a clustering diagram, follow this procedure:

- Write a word or phrase that seems to focus on what you want to write about. For example, write "acid rain" in the middle of a page and circle it.

- Connect supporting ideas to your circled phrase by drawing a line from the phrase to the related concepts. Circle and connect each aspect of acid rain back to the central idea.

- To expand further, draw possible clusters from each of the subclusters, in this way finding ever more detailed ideas to work with.

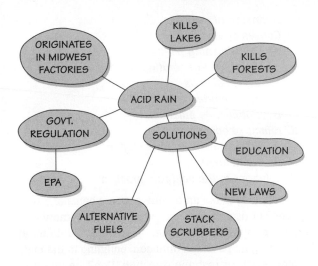

10 | *Outlining to Organize Ideas*

Outlines are organized lists. They are a powerful way to begin and advance a writing project—so long as you understand that you can modify the outline when new and better ideas emerge. To make an outline, start with an idea and then see how many questions you can ask about it. If you start with "acid rain," ask yourself, *What is it? What causes it? What are its effects? How can it be stopped?* Once you have such a list, arrange answers in a progression that makes sense, throwing out those that don't fit and adding others as they seem relevant.

Formal outlines follow a few guidelines to establish hierarchy (major versus minor ideas) and logic (which ideas depend on which). Use Roman numerals for major headings, capital letters for supporting ones, and Arabic numbers for still smaller ideas. Keep parallel ideas in parallel grammatical form (e.g., use all noun clusters or all complete sentences, but be consistent).

In the following example, the four main points are designated with Roman numerals; the supporting ideas, with capital letters; and the smaller details, with Arabic numbers.

I.   Definition of acid rain
II. Causes of acid rain
   A.   Coal-burning plants
      1.   Power-generating stations
      2.   Steel mills
      3.   Factories
   B.   Automobile pollution
III. Effects of acid rain
   A.   Deforestation in New England
   B.   Dead lakes
IV. Solutions to the acid rain problem

The effort to make an outline not only helps organize the paper but also shows you what you don't know and where your supporting information is weak. Outlining at the beginning helps shape direction; outlining in the middle helps retain or reshape direction. Don't be afraid to modify or scrap initial outlines when your thoughts take you in new and better directions.

11 | *Asking Questions to Test Ideas*

Reporters train themselves to ask six basic questions to make sure they include all necessary information in the news stories they are writing: *Who? What? Where? When? Why? How?* Applying these same questions to your own writing will remind you to include all useful information as well as prompt you to generate new ideas in your text. To test the completeness of your personal or academic writing, ask yourself the reporter's questions:

- Who was involved?
- What happened?
- Where did this happen?
- When did it happen?
- Why did it happen?
- How did it happen?

Asking these questions about a first or second draft will tell you if you have included all the relevant information or left something out. In other words, it helps to ask reporter's questions both at the beginning and at the end of your writing.

PART three
Writing College Papers

Academic papers are assigned for a variety of purposes that vary according to discipline, instructor, situation, and writer intention. Whether a paper presents information, explains ideas, supports a thesis, or explores ideas, the form, organization, style, and mechanics should be consistent with that purpose. The only guarantee of logical and formal consistency in academic papers is careful revision (see Chapters 15–16).

12   *Finding Direction in Academic Papers*

Purpose shapes a writer's questions, approach, research, organizing strategies, form, and voice. For the sake of brevity, we look at three common purposes behind college papers: *informing, persuading,* and *expressing.* But note that writing any paper often includes multiple purposes, not all of which may be discussed here. For example, while the larger intent of a paper may be persuasion, you may want to include expressive or informative passages to help accomplish that end.

12 a   Writing to inform

Informative writing can be about any subject—literary, historical, and philosophical ideas; the results of laboratory and survey experiments; how-to demonstrations; and so on. The focus is on *information* rather than on *audience* or *writer;* consequently, the language in such reports is usually neutral, excluding personal opinion, bias, and first-person pronouns as much as possible. Standard strategies of presenting information include explaining, defining, describing, classifying and dividing, comparing and contrasting, and analyzing causes and effects. Common forms include laboratory and book reports as well as research papers.

- An informational report usually reveals its purpose in its title and in the introduction on the first page. If the report includes an informational thesis, that too is usually revealed on the first page. Such papers sometimes include an abstract after the title page, summarizing the paper's main points. This up-front focus on purpose helps readers hone in on the information being presented.

12 b   Writing to persuade

Persuasive writing attempts to convince readers that one idea, interpretation, product, or argument is better than another. An effective persuasive paper convinces the reader that the writer's claim is true. The information and personal beliefs expressed in it assure your reader that what you say has merit. Persuasive papers focus on the *audience* more than either *subject* or *writer;* they ask you to argue, interpret, convince, defend, debate, or make a case for or against something. Forms include position papers, critical or interpretive essays, editorials, reviews, and any paper that requires taking a stand and backing it up.

■ Persuasion or argument papers commonly include a thesis that directly and succinctly states the author's main point. The thesis statement sometimes comes at the beginning (the rest of the paper supports it) or sometimes is delayed until the end (both sides have now been examined, and one is more persuasive than the other).

12 c Writing to express

Expressive or personal writing reveals how the author thinks or feels about something and commonly raises more questions than it answers. Formally assigned papers that invite authors to express their personal ideas are often called *essays* (from the French verb *essayer,* "to attempt") that explore, speculate about, or reflect on a given question, issue, or text. Such expressive essays commonly focus as much on the quality of the *writer's* mind and voice as on the *subject* or *audience.* The meaning or point of such essays is as likely to be speculative or ambiguous as conclusive.

■ Expressive essays commonly examine, explore, or imply a thesis rather than state or support one in a definitive manner.

13 Making Claims in Academic Papers

The reason for writing academic papers is often to answer questions that are either stated or implied. Even a simple report explaining the principle of "lift" on airplane wings answers a question about how airplanes fly. An interpretive essay arguing in favor of cultural diversity answers a question about the value of cultural diversity. In many college papers, both in English classes and across the curriculum, the answer to such questions is called a *thesis.* If you are required to write a thesis–driven paper, make sure you know what a thesis is, where you want it to appear, and how to state it in a convincing manner.

13 a Thesis statements

Although the whole text of a sharply focused paper explains or argues its thesis, both informative and argument papers benefit from stating the paper's main point in a single sentence, called a **thesis statement.** Articulating your thesis on the first page makes clear to readers where the paper is going and what the rest of the paper will explain, argue, support, or defend. Articulating the thesis at the paper's end after exploring both sides of an issue leaves no doubt about where you stand.

When you begin to write, it helps to formulate a **working thesis** to focus your quest for an answer. As you research and write, both your question and your thesis may change—a good sign, because it means that you are learning something you didn't already know. For example, to begin writing a paper on cultural diversity, you might ask this question:

■ **Question:** *How can Northfield College attract more minority students to increase cultural diversity on campus?*

To address this question—to which you do not know the answer—you make a good guess, which we'll call a *hypothesis* or *working thesis.* Your guess should (1) suggest a possible real answer and (2) be doable in the time and with the resources available. Make this tentative assertion as specific as your current knowledge allows.

■ **Working thesis:** *To attract minority students, Northfield College needs to create a more culturally diverse campus environment.*

At this point in starting the paper, you have only a hunch about what the answer might be. Further research, however, convinces you that faculty diversity is the key to student diversity, so your paper's final thesis becomes the following:

■ **Thesis statement:** *Northfield College will attract minority students if it hires minority faculty to teach them.*

A good strategy for academic papers is to include the thesis statement on the first page, preferably at the end of a first paragraph that poses the problem the paper will address. In this way, your instructor knows right away the purpose of your paper and will read to see if that purpose is achieved. Here, for example, is the first paragraph for the Northfield College paper:

> Recent racial incidents among students in the dormitories at Northfield College have called attention to the homogeneous nature of the students, who, like the faculty, are largely white and of European ancestry. Current students, supported by the trustees and faculty, have called for increased efforts to recruit minority students in the belief that this would decrease racial tension. But how are minority students to be recruited to an all-white campus? This paper argues that Northfield College will attract more minority students if it hires minority faculty to teach them.

13 b Claims and counterclaims

The main point made by academic papers is called a thesis (stated or implied), but it could also be called its major **claim.** Likewise, each point in support of that overall claim can be called a minor claim. Simply put, a claim is an assertion or statement that something is true or should be done. This chapter proposes a simple process for making and sequencing claims; the following section explains how to support them.

Finding a Topic

A common academic assignment requires you to write an argument or position paper about a controversial topic or issue. Start this paper by selecting an issue that interests you and that also meets the following criteria:

■ It is controversial.

■ It has two distinct, arguable, and realistic positions.

■ Resources are available to support both sides.

Consider the difference between national versus local topics: National topics, such as homeland security or universal health care, are widely reported in the major news media and well documented in the university library and on the Internet. Local topics, such as mountain biking in Riverside Park or cultural diversity at Northfield College, will provide places to visit and experts to interview. Our sample topic is both national (mountain biking in wilderness areas) and local (a proposal to ban mountain biking in Riverside Park)—a guarantee of rich and varied research sources:

- Should mountain biking be allowed in Riverside Park?

Making Claims

Once you've selected an issue and chosen which side to support, use research and careful reasoning to make a list of all the claims that support your side of the argument—you're not writing the paper yet, just preparing the outline. Here, for example, are the claims to support mountain biking in Riverside Park:

- All people should have the right to use the park so long as they do not damage it.
- A Sierra Club study found that mountain bike tires are less harmful to forest trails than lug-soled hiking boots.
- Most mountain bike riders are respectful of the environment and courteous to other trail users.

Making Counterclaims

Statements that present the other side of an issue are called **counterclaims.** Once the claims are listed, list the counterclaims that challenge your position:

- Mountain bike riders ride fast and are sometimes reckless.
- Mountain bike tires damage trails and cause erosion.

After listing the counterclaims, you can conclude your paper by refuting them or arguing that your claims are more valid.

Writing the Paper

Before you finish writing this position paper, you have one more strategic decision to make: Do you want to lead with your thesis so that readers know where you stand from the start, or do you want to delay stating your thesis and keep the readers in suspense?

There are three advantages to leading with a thesis:
(1) The audience always knows where you stand. (2) The
thesis occupies both emphatic positions in a paper, first
and last. (3) Thesis-first is the expected form of academic
argument in many disciplines.

There are also three advantages to a delayed-thesis argument: (1) You show your audience both sides of the issue.
(2) Being kept in suspense increases reader interest in fin-
ishing the paper. (3) The audience understands your difficulty in making a decision.

14 Using Evidence in Academic Writing

When you write papers that make claims about what
is true, the following sources can be counted on to
provide believable evidence: *facts, examples, inferences,
expert opinion,* and *personal experience.*

Facts are verifiable and agreed on by everyone, regardless of personal beliefs or values. It is a fact that water
boils at 212 degrees Fahrenheit. It is a fact that Northfield
College employed three black faculty members in 2004. It
is a fact that Riverside Park is adjacent to the western
boundary of the college campus. Facts are often numerical
or statistical and are recorded where readers can look them
up in a dictionary, almanac, public report, college catalog,
or atlas.

"Near facts" may be another category that most rea-
sonable people would subscribe to, although means of proof
are more questionable: Mount Hood is a tall mountain, Milwaukee is a large city, French is a romantic language.

Examples illustrate a claim or clarify an issue. To explain that many wilderness trails remain closed to mountain biking, report those so listed by the National Park
Service.

Inferences are generalizations based on the accumu-
lation of facts and examples. For instance, if you check three
city parks and find that they are all open to mountain biking, you might infer a city policy supporting that sport in
city parks. But such an inference is not a fact because you
have not checked all the city parks or checked with the
department that sets park policies.

Expert opinion makes powerful evidence. When a forest ranger testifies about trail damage caused by mountain bikes or lug-soled hiking boots, his training and experience make him an expert. A casual hiker making the same observation is less believable.

Personal experience is testimony based on firsthand knowledge. If you have ridden mountain bikes in Riverside Park for two years, your knowledge cannot easily be discounted.

15 | *Guidelines for Revision*

Learning to write is learning to rewrite, which happens in two distinct stages: (1) **revising,** the primary way of developing a paper's ideas and direction, and (2) **editing,** the primary way of polishing and refining its sentences (the final stage of editing, **proofreading,** detects errors in spelling, typing, grammar, and punctuation).

Revising means seeing the topic, thesis, claims, evidence, organization, or conclusion through new eyes—your own after putting it aside for a while and critical friends who see things you missed. It means making changes to modify the paper's content, direction, and meaning. There is no single way to revise, but the following strategies may help.

■ Compose all drafts on a computer so that you can add, delete, and move blocks of text easily before you are done.

■ Create self-imposed due dates earlier than the instructor's due date to guarantee you'll have time to revise and edit.

■ Let a first draft sit overnight; the next day, you'll see more clearly what works well, what doesn't, and where to make changes.

■ If you make a change in one place, it may have repercussions elsewhere in the paper. Review everything.

■ Ask readers you trust about the strength of your thesis, the credibility of your evidence, and the clarity of your point.

■ Read your paper out loud. Does it sound like you—your commitments and voice? If not, revise until it does.

- Sticking with tedious topics, false directions, or old language hinders creative and critical thinking. Be willing to scrap and start fresh.

---

16 | *Experiments with Revision*

You can bring new life to a paper by challenging yourself to see it in new ways. Consider these possibilities for refocusing your work: (1) *Limit* focus or scope, (2) *add* new material, (3) *switch* perspective, and (4) *transform* the genre. These experiments work equally well with informative, persuasive, and expressive papers.

Limit

Early drafts often cover too much ground in too few pages so that depth, detail, and development are lost.

- Limit your second draft to one idea in a single paragraph of your first draft.
- Limit your second draft to "real time" so that the action in your paper happens in the time it takes to read it.
- Limit your second draft to a single setting in which meaningful dialogue or action occurs.

Add

Drafts get stale when writers keep rehashing the same ideas. Make a resolution to add new information with each revision.

- Add local people. Find a local expert to interview and quote in your paper.
- Add re-created dialogue by visualizing an experience and employing language that approximates the occasion.
- Add library and Internet sources to teach readers more than you knew when you started writing.

Switch

Revitalize drafts by switching your point of view. You don't need to stay "switched" for more than a draft, but this experiment lets you witness the story afresh.

- Switch point of view (first versus third person), verb tense (past versus present), style, or voice (formal versus colloquial) to present your ideas from a different perspective.
- Switch audience by writing a draft to a distant friend to see how changing audience changes your language.
- Switch from exposition to narrative or vice versa. Narrate the story of your search instead of simply reporting its results.

Transform

Experiment with a new form or genre. You will not know the full effect of a new form until you actually create it; it might be a pleasant surprise.

- Transform within nonfiction genres: Rewrite a personal essay as a journal, diary, or letter exchange. Recast a research paper as a feature article or as talk-show dialogue.
- Transform to creative genres: Instead of prose, write verse; instead of narrative, write drama.
- Transform to a form that complements and enhances the content of the paper.

When you try any of these experiments, treat the content of the paper just as seriously as if you wrote in a more conventional mode. To be safe, check with your instructor before turning in a creative final draft.

WRITING ACROSS THE CURRICULUM

Imagining Revision

Review the examples below and invent your own imaginatively focused version of a paper you need to write somewhere across the curriculum.

Art history: Review a local art exhibit in the form that might appear in both the local and campus newspapers.

Biology: Write a science fiction story in the fashion of your own favorite author, book, or movie; include carefully researched biological facts and principles, but take one imaginative leap (fiction, not fact) that creates a problem for your local community.

Business: Invent a case study for a new product including perspectives from several corporate points of view (marketing manager, CEO, technical support) as well as several consumers with realistic but colorful complaints.

Communications: Recreate a fictional television talk-show interview from perspectives similar to those of a Jon Stewart or a Rush Limbaugh interviewing an expert about a critical issue in contemporary communications.

Education: Write an editorial supporting a local school-board decision with a major impact on local schools; then write half a dozen letters-to-the-editor in response to the editorial.

Geology: Interview the survivor of a natural disaster such as a forest fire, flood, tornado, or drought; then research the same event on the Internet and in the library. Write an account of this event as it might appear in *Time* or *Newsweek* magazine.

History: Adopt the role of an important historical figure and compose a fictive letter exchange between this figure and his or her historical nemesis.

Literature: Invent the missing chapter or compose an alternative ending for a literary work you are studying in your English class; be sure to replicate the style and form of the work, and make your new content consistent with the content and theme of the original.

Political science: Write a public opinion column on a troublesome political issue in the style of a syndicated columnist representing a particular point of view, such as conservative George F. Will or liberal Ellen Goodman; conclude with letters to the editor sparked by the column.

Psychology: Contrast two major psychological theorists by sitting them down in a coffee shop (or bar or mall or talk-show debate) for a conversation about a current issue of some psychological importance.

Sociology: Write an advice column as commonly published in newspapers in response to a question of some social concern in the fashion of Dear Abby or Ann Landers.

PART four

Research Writing

A research project begins with a question that (1) interests you, (2) doesn't have an easy answer, and (3) can be examined in the time and with the resources available. If you have a tentative answer to your question, formulate a working thesis to help guide your research (see Chapter 13). If research leads to more questions or suggests a more interesting topic, redirect your investigation and revise your working thesis.

17 | *Planning Research*

17 a Start with questions

To begin an independent research project, ask the following questions: What investigations would match course goals? Which investigation am I most interested in? What sources are available? How much time do I have? Why would anyone else care about the results?

Limit the Topic

Limit your topic to a manageable scope and size. Instead of trying to analyze all the fiction of Alice Walker, limit the topic first to a book you want to investigate, say *The Color Purple;* then decide what specific aspect of the novel to investigate—the development of a specific character? a particular theme? the historical setting? and so on.

Own the Topic

Conducting research means entering an ongoing conversation with a select community of people who are knowledgeable about a subject. To enter the conversation, put the facts and ideas you collect into your own words at every chance—in a research log, on note cards, in rough drafts. Finding your own language guarantees that you understand the idea and increases your chances of saying something useful, interesting, or provocative.

17 b Keep a research log

The best way to start and manage a research project is to keep a research log—a daily journal of your investigation—to both discover a topic and keep track of the research project as you pose questions, track down answers, eliminate false leads, take source notes, and modify the project's direction.

Writing as you research forces you to articulate ideas and examine supporting evidence critically—which, in turn, helps you focus your research activities. Following is a brief sample from a research log investigating ozone holes in the atmosphere.

11/12   Checked the subject headings—found no books on ozone depletion. Ref. librarian suggests looking at magazines because books take much longer to get published. Found twenty articles in the General Science Index—got printouts on about half. Start obtaining the sources and reading them tomorrow.

11/17   Conference today with professor about the ozone-hole thesis—said I didn't really have much of a thesis yet, just a lot of notes on the same subject. I should look at what I've got, then step back and decide what question it answers—that will probably point to my thesis.

17 c   Focus on a question

Research projects are designed to answer questions the answers to which you do not already know. A good research question meets the following criteria:

- You find it personally interesting.
- You don't already know the answer.
- You have the time and resources to track down the answer.

17 d   Attempt an answer

To research in a specific direction, formulate a working thesis—a tentative answer to the question you plan to pursue. Essentially, it's a hunch or an educated guess to guide your investigation. If more research leads in a different direction—and you're interested in this new direction—redirect your investigation and revise your thesis. (See 13a.)

For an informational report, begin with an open mind (What would be the effects of legalizing marijuana?) and find out background information about your topic before you commit to a single answer (Legalizing marijuana would be a disaster—or maybe not). In other words, when you don't have a thesis in mind, informational research can help you find one, at which point your paper can either present the information you found in a neutral manner (There are both pros and cons to legalizing marijuana) or make an argument favoring one idea over another.

In contrast, if you begin a research project with a thesis already in mind (Legalizing marijuana for medical purposes is a good idea), you'll spend most of your time locating evidence to support and strengthen your position. However, be open to the possibility that your research could change your thesis because it's difficult to write a convincing paper when you, the writer, no longer believe in your position.

17 e Use the writing process

Take your research through all the stages of the writing process: plan, investigate, draft, revise, and edit. At the same time, note that research writing presents a few special problems.

Plan

The technical requirements of research writing—length, format, the nature and number of the sources, and precise documentation—require library and online research and, perhaps, site visits and interviews. In addition, plan time for writing, revising, and editing.

Find Sources

To evaluate sources, learn the difference between *primary* and *secondary* sources. Primary sources contain original material and/or raw information. Secondary sources report on, describe, interpret, or analyze someone else's work. If you explore the development of a novelist's style, for example, the novels themselves are primary sources. Other people's reviews and interpretations of the novels are secondary sources. Primary sources ground a paper in first-hand observations and facts; secondary sources supply context and support for your own analysis and argument.

Draft

Write your first draft early to allow time for further research. When you try to articulate a first or tentative answer to your research question, it may prove faulty. The way to find the fault is to write; the way to fix the fault is to research further and write again. Many research essays present the thesis statement at the beginning, in the first or second paragraph, where it establishes what will follow. Some research papers delay the thesis statement until the end, where it acts as a conclusion or a summary. If you take the delayed-thesis approach, be sure that the topic and scope of your paper are clear to your readers in the beginning paragraphs. (See 13b.)

Revise

Revising may entail modifying both the writing and the research that underlies it. Once research begins, your questions and answers multiply and change. Be prepared to find new questions more interesting to you than your original question. Remember, the act of writing—both informal and formal—focuses the brain: the more you write, the better you focus.

Edit

Editing and proofreading require extra time as you need to check the writing, the information, and the documentation. The editing stage is a good time to assess your use of quotation, paraphrase, and summary to make sure you have not misquoted or used a source without crediting it.

---

18 | *Conducting Library Research*

The college library is the heart of the academic community and the most reliable source of credible information in all academic subjects. Many informative resources are also available on the Internet and in the field, though their reliability varies immensely. In contrast, resources screened by professional librarians for authenticity and credibility are likely to be reliable. Librarians can save you precious time by showing you the most helpful resources. If you are not sure how to begin, follow this research plan.

18 a Learn the library

To take full advantage of library resources, keep the following suggestions in mind:

- Visit early and often. Begin your research by physically visiting the library, becoming comfortable with how it works, and locate the catalogue, book stacks, reference room, and circulation desk.
- Survey the catalogue. Find out what resources are available for your project. Even if your initial research

indicates a wealth of material, you may not be able to find everything the first time, so resolve to come back.

- Check general sources first. Look at dictionaries, encyclopedias, atlases, and yearbooks for background information. An hour spent with general sources will provide a quick overview of the scope and range of your topic and suggest leads to more specific information.

- Ask for help. Talk to librarians. Show them your assignment; describe your tentative topic; ask for research suggestions. Librarians are professional information experts, so use them.

18 b Find information

Most of the information you need to find will be contained in reference books, in other books, and in periodicals (journals, magazines, and newspapers). To locate these sources, use the online catalog and databases as well as periodical indexes. To use these resources efficiently, use the following process:

Consult General Reference Works

Use databases (also called indexes) to locate general reference sources to material published within periodicals (magazines, journals, newspapers published at set periods throughout the year). A keyword search will turn up information more current than found in books. Select the particular index or database that contains journals, magazines, and newspapers relevant to your project.

Full-text databases allow you to print out the full text of an article. But beware: some texts are abbreviated when they are stored on the computer, others omit sidebars or graphics, and some cost money to be retrieved. If a database listing looks important, but is not retrievable in full text form, search for the periodical (paper or electronic version) and read the article. The following databases may prove especially useful:

- Academic Search Premier. Indexes over 3,400 scholarly publications, including humanities, sciences, social sciences, education, engineering, languages, and literature, full-text.

- ArticleFirst. Indexes over 15,000 journals in business, humanities, medicine, science, and social science.

- Expanded Academic ASAP. Indexes over 2,000 periodicals in the arts, humanities, sciences, and social sciences, as well as many newspapers.

- Factiva. Full-text access to major newspapers, business journals, and stock market reports.

- LexisNexis Academic. Indexes a wide range of magazines, newspapers, and government documents, full-text.

Consult Specialized Reference Works

Use online databases to search for specialized reference works that contain articles by well-known authorities and sometimes have bibliographies and cross-references that can lead to other sources. Access is usually restricted, so consult a reference librarian to see which databases are available for your use.

A major online system commonly found in college libraries is Dialog, offering more than 400 specialized databases, including the following:

- Arts and Humanities Search (1980–present),

- ERIC (Educational Resources Information Center, 1966–present),

- MLA International Bibliography (1963–present),

- PsycINFO (1967–present), Scisearch (1974–present),

- Social Scisearch (1972–present).

Consult the Online Catalog

All catalogs list items by author, title, and subject; describe their physical format and content, and tell where in the library to find them. Consult the online catalog to find all books, journals, newspapers, and audiovisual material the library owns. Most online catalogs can be accessed from locations outside the library.

If you already know the title of a work, the catalog confirms availability. If it's not in your library, use the World Wide Web to locate it in other libraries, where your library can possibly obtain it through an interlibrary loan, a process that may take anywhere from a few days to a few weeks.

Most online catalogs allow you to perform keyword searches, allowing the computer to search different parts

What You Need to Know About Keyword Searching

When you are looking for materials on a particular topic, a keyword search is often your best bet. A keyword search is a comprehensive way to search and tells the computer to look for your word or words anywhere in a record—in the title, the author name, the subject headings, the journal title, or the abstract. Keyword searching allows you to combine terms in different ways using Boolean connectors to either broaden or narrow your search results. Truncation is another powerful keyword searching tool that allows you to add greater flexibility to your searches by telling the computer to search for variant word endings. Both techniques are described below.

BOOLEAN CONNECTORS

▶ **BOOLEAN CONNECTORS**

Boolean Connector		Examples	Search Result
	and	forests and vermont wetlands and ecology	Retrieves records containing *both* terms; *narrows* the search.
	or	lakes or ponds color or colour	Retrieves records containing *either or both* terms; *broadens* a search.
	not	vermont not new hampshire	*Excludes* records containing the second term; *narrows* the search.

TRUNCATION

Truncation	Example	Search Result
Use a truncation symbol at the end of a word or a root word, and the computer will search for all its different word endings. Different databases use different symbols (?, *, |, or #), so check the online help to learn what symbol to use.	environment*	*The use of "*" retrieves. . .* environment environmental environmentalist environmentalists environmentalism environmentally environments

of the record at once. To perform a keyword search, use the words you've identified as describing your topic, linked by "and" or "or" as appropriate. For example, if you're trying to research fictional accounts of Dakota Indians, you can search for "Dakota Indians" AND "fiction." The computer will present you with a list of works that fit that description.

Two "meta-library" search tools that allow searches of multiple card catalogs simultaneously are LibWebCats http://www.librarytechnology.org/libwebcats/ and Libdex www.libdex.com.

Consult Other Sources of Information

Government documents. The U.S. government publishes numerous reports, pamphlets, catalogs, and newsletters on most issues of national concern. Consult the Monthly Catalogue of United States Government Publications and the United States Government Publications Index, both available electronically.

Nonprint media. Records, CDs, audiocassettes, videotapes, slides, photographs, and other media may also be located through the library catalog.

Pamphlets. Pamphlets and brochures published by government agencies and private organizations are generally stored in a library's vertical file. The Vertical File Index: A Subject and Title Index to Selected Pamphlet Material (1932/35–present) lists many of the available titles. Many are also available via the World Wide Web.

Special collections. Rare books, manuscripts, and items of local interest are commonly found in a special room or section of the library.

Maps and geographic information systems (GIS). Maps and atlases depict much more than roads and state boundaries, including information on population density, language patterns, soil types, and much more.

18 c   Take good notes

Taking careful notes is imperative, enabling you to locate, remember, and use sources effectively in your writing. Either a card-based system or laptop computer works well. Two kinds of notes are especially useful.

- **Bibliographic notes.** A bibliographic note identifies the source, not its content. When you locate a useful source, record the information necessary to find it again on a 3-by-5 index card or computer equivalent; use a separate "card" for each work as soon as you find each source, even before taking notes from the source. Creating bibliographic notes as you go and then arranging them in alphabetical order allows you to prepare the Reference page required at the end of academic papers. (For complete bibliographic information appropriate for each discipline, see documentation conventions in Chapters 26–38.)

- **Information notes.** Record the relevant information from every source consulted. Focus each note on your research question, so their relevance is clear when read later. We recommend 4-by-6 index cards (or electronic equivalent) for informational notes. Each card should contain only one piece of information or one idea to allow easy arrangement in outline form as you write. The top of each note card identifies author and title, with full bibliographic identification on the bibliographic cards (see above). Include page numbers for all quoted or paraphrased material.

WRITING ACROSS THE CURRICULUM

Suggestions for Talking with Librarians

The following suggestions apply to any research situation in any discipline where the writer wants to advance the research project and learn more about the way libraries work.

- Bring with you a copy of the research assignment and be prepared to describe the course/discipline for which you are conducting the research. Also bring along a copy of the course syllabus.

- Be ready to explain the assignment in your own words: purpose, format, length, number of sources, and due date.

- Identify any special requirements about sources: Should information come from government documents? rare books? films?

- Describe the particular topic you are researching and the tentative question you have framed to address the topic.

- Describe any work you have done so far: Web sites, books, or periodicals looked at; log entries written; people interviewed; and so on.

- Think about it this way: Reference librarians don't like to sit around with nothing to do. The more difficult the questions, the more interesting their work.

19 | Conducting Internet Research

Most college research projects will involve some Internet sources; few projects should rely on them entirely. And although you probably are familiar with Google, Yahoo!, and MSN Search, for college writing you will need search tools that focus less on consumer goods and popular culture and more on resources that are useful to students and other academic writers.

19 a   Identify search tools

Budget time just to explore search resources, identifying ones that cover your subject. No single site catalogues the entire Web, and no two engines search exactly the same way. Try the same search phrases on different sites and several different searches on each site. When you're not in a hurry, the best approach is "trial and error."

Depending on your topic, you may find one search engine much more useful than others. Here are a few academic search sites, each of which can lead to many others.

- WorldCat, http://www.oclc.org/worldcat/. The nonprofit Online Computer Library Center search engine locates books and other materials through a network of worldwide library catalogs.

- Library of Congress Online Catalog, http://catalog.loc .gov/. Access to the most comprehensive collection of materials in the United States.

- The Internet Public Library, http://www.ipl.org/. Maintained by the University of Michigan School of Information.

- University of Wisconsin Internet Scout, http://scout.wisc.edu/. Finds and lists academic resources with emphasis on science, mathematics, technology, and engineering.

- Applied Math and Science Education Repository, http://amser.org/.

- Infomine, http://infomine.ucr.edu/. A broad academic directory operated by the University of California at Riverside.

- Librarians' Index to the Internet, http://www.lii.org/. A directory to resources compiled by public librarians.

- Academic Info, http://www.academicinfo.net/. A comprehensive directory site covering many fields.

- RefDesk.com, http://www.refdesk.com/. A site dedicated to research of all kinds.

- Reference.com, http://www.reference.com/. A listing of dictionaries, thesauruses, encyclopedias, and more.

19 b Limit your search

First searches usually provide too much information—sometimes several thousand (or million!) sites—making it hard to locate items you can use. For example, a single search term such as "Vietnam" may locate thousands of articles from travel information to news to geography and language—too many to explore.

  If you search on the term Vietnam War, many search engines will retrieve a list of sites that contain only one of the two search words—thus some will be about Vietnam, but not the war; others about war, but not Vietnam. Again, too many sites. Here's how to fix this:

- Use quotation marks to limit a specific phrase, title, or name by putting the words in double quotation marks around the whole phrase, "Vietnam War," or a book title, "The Best and the Brightest," or an author, "David Halberstam." This limits the site selection to those that include both words.

- Use "and" between words to limit the search to sources that include both terms (not already combined in a phrase). Typing crime and punishment (on some sites, crime + punishment) will return documents that include both words, whereas using quotation marks will get you Crime and Punishment, the novel by Dostoevsky.

- Use "or" between words to retrieve documents that include any, rather than all, of the search words. Example: puma or mountain lion or cougar or panther.

- Use "not" after a term to exclude a word that must not appear in the documents. Example: dolphins not football.

- Use an asterisk* to substitute for letters or word endings that might vary: parent* for parents, parental, or parenting.

- Use parentheses ( ) to group and combine search expressions: "(treaty or armistice) and Korean War."

You can nest several phrases within a query: (treaty or armistice) and Korea and (war or police action) and "Douglas MacArthur."

Each search engine uses slightly different coding for the same underlying concepts; consult the "advanced search" or "search help" links for specifics.

19 c Tips

- Find elusive Web pages. Specific articles sometimes move or disappear from Web sites. If the address for a specific article yields only an error message, check your typing and try again. If you still get an error message, shorten the URL to take you to a page on the site. For example, if you can't find the article http://www.capitalcommunitynews.com/ publications/ eotr/2006-AUGUST/HTML/Is_Pepco_Linked.cfm, try http://www.capitalcommunitynews.com/publications/ eotr/2006-AUGUST/HTML/ or http://www.capital communitynews.com/. Then search that site for the article in question.

- Document your search. It can be difficult to retrace your steps to a valuable resource. Use notecards or a word-processing file to keep track of which search engines and which search terms you use so you can reproduce a search easily. When you find a useful Web page, print a copy for your records. If your browser doesn't automatically do so, write the URL of the page on your printout along with the date and time you accessed the page. Copy the URL into your research notes.

19 d Search with e-mail

Once you have an e-mail address, you can correspond with millions of other people who have useful research information. To locate an e-mail address, try Search.com at http://www.search.com/search?channel=10 or an address metasearch at http://www.addresses.com. People often post their e-mail addresses on their own Web sites, and institutions such as universities often have faculty e-mail directories on their Web pages. If you know someone who works at an institution but can't find his or her e-mail address, try writing to the contact address provided on the Web site.

19 e Document your search

In a research log or notebook, record search terms you use, sites you visit, and e-mail contacts. Print copies of useful pages or information, and if your printer doesn't automatically print Web URLs, record them as well as the date and time in your notebook. If you're using your own computer, save useful locations in your browser's Bookmark or Favorites file.

20 | Conducting Field Research

Depending on your research question, you may need to conduct research outside the library and away from the computer. Field research simply means visiting places (a lakeshore, a city) or people (a biologist, a worker) and taking careful notes. Field research gets you fresh, local information about people, places, events, or objects to provide you with original data to incorporate into research papers.

20 a Site observation tips

The following suggestions will increase your chances of successful site visits.

- Select relevant sites. When doing research at local sites, visit places that will be the primary focus of your paper or offer supplementary details to support your major points.

- Do homework. Consult reference room or online sources such as encyclopedias, dictionaries, and atlases to orient you toward and inform yourself about the places you will visit.

- Call ahead. Find out directions and convenient times to visit and let site people know you are coming.

- Bring a notebook with a stiff cover. It will help you write while walking or standing. Double-entry notebooks allow you to record facts in one column and your reactions in the other.

- Use a handheld tape recorder for on-site dictation to supplement or replace written notes.

- Review, transcribe, and rewrite both written and dictated notes within twenty-four hours after your visit.

- Sketch, photograph, or videotape useful visual information.

20 b Interview tips

The following suggestions will increase your chances for successful personal interviews.

- Select relevant people. Determine what information you need, who is likely to have it, and how to approach them.

- Call ahead for an appointment. Let your subject know when you are coming or when appointments need changing.

- Do homework. Consult library or Internet sources for background information on your interview subject.

- Prepare questions in advance. Ask general questions to establish context; ask specific questions to become more informed.

- Ask open questions to elicit general information: How did that situation develop? What are your plans for the future?

- Ask closed questions when you need facts or concrete details to support a point: When did that policy begin? What is the name of the district manager?

- Ask follow-up questions if answers are incomplete or confusing. Get all the information possible at one sitting.

- Use silence. If your subject does not respond right away, allow time for him or her to think, recall, or reflect before filling the silence with another question.

- Read body language. Notice how your subject acts: Does the person look you in the eyes? Fidget? Look bored? Smile? These are actions that suggest whether someone is speaking honestly, avoiding your question, or tiring fast. Including descriptions of body language along with conversation adds interest to your paper.

- Use a tape recorder. Ask permission in advance, and make sure your equipment works. Continue to make written notes of conversation highlights to help you remember questions that occur while your subject is talking and to describe the subject's appearance and manner.

- Confirm important assertions. Read back important or controversial statements to check for accuracy and allow for further explanation.

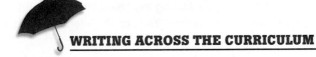

WRITING ACROSS THE CURRICULUM

The Role of the Researcher in Field Research

The researcher is present, one way or another, in all research projects, but never more so than in field research. When using textual sources such as books, articles, Web sites, and pamphlets, the researcher is able to rely on language created by other people to credit, discredit, or question. However, in field research, the researcher plays a larger role in creating the language of the source. In other words, the researcher participates directly in both the creation and the evaluation of interview and site-visit material used in writing research essays.

- The researcher directly shapes interview material through (1) the questions asked, (2) the site chosen, and (3) the language in which notes are taken.

- The researcher shapes on-site material by selecting the site, by placing a camera in one place and not another, and by selecting what to focus on and what to ignore. In like manner, the location and audio level of a tape recorder affect what is heard and what is not.

- The researcher assigns value to the field sources through the way they are collected (notes, tapes, photos) as well as how they are recorded, developed, transcribed, and saved.

Account for your preparation, participation, and perspective in any field research that you have undertaken sometime in the recent past, which may include a chemistry experiment, a geology laboratory, an author interview, a natural resources field trip, an art class drawing expedition, or a sociological survey.

21 | *Evaluating Research Sources*

G ood sources inform your papers and make them believable. To determine that a source is good, you must be able to answer "yes" to two questions: (1) Is the source credible? and (2) Is it useful in my paper? This chapter provides guidelines for evaluating the credibility and usefulness of sources found in the library, on the Internet, and in the field.

21 a   Evaluating library sources

The sources found in a college library are generally credible because experts have already screened them. The books, periodicals, documents, special collections, and electronic sources have been recommended for library acquisition by scholars, researchers, and librarians with special expertise in the subject areas the library catalogs. However, just because some authorities judged a source to be credible at one time does not necessarily mean it still is or that it's the best available or that it's not contested or that it's especially useful for the paper you are writing. Two of the main reasons for distrusting a source found in the library have to do with time (when was it judged true?) and perspective (who said it was true, and for what reason?).

Identify Dated Sources

Most library documents include their date of publication inside the cover of the document itself, and in most cases this will be a fact you can rely on. In some cases, such as articles first published in one place and reprinted in an anthology, you may have to dig for the original date, but it's usually there (check the permissions page).

One of the main reasons any source may become unreliable—and less than credible—is the passage of time. For example, any geographical, political, or statistical information true for 1950 or even 2004 will be more or less changed by the time you examine it—in many cases, radically so. (Just look at atlas or encyclopedia entries for Africa or Asia from 1950!) Yet at one time this source was judged to be accurate.

Check the critical reception of books when published by reading reviews in *Book Review Digest* (also available online); often you can tell whether the critical argument over the book twenty years ago is still relevant or has been bypassed by other events and publications.

At the same time, dated information has all sorts of uses. In spite of being "dated," works such as the Bible, the I Ching, the novels of Virginia Woolf, and the beliefs of Malcolm X are valuable for many reasons. In studying change over time, old statistical information is crucial. Knowing the source date lets you decide whether to use it.

Identify Perspective

Who created the source, and with what intention? Why did the person or organization write, construct, compile, record, or otherwise create this source in the first place? This second question is difficult to answer by reviewing the source itself. Although most library texts include the dates they were published, few accurately advertise their purpose or the author's point of view—and when they do, this information cannot always be believed.

To evaluate the usefulness of a text, ask questions about (1) the assumptions it makes, (2) the evidence it presents, and (3) the reasoning that holds it together. Finding answers to these critical questions reveals an author's bias:

- What is this writer's purpose—scholarly analysis, political advocacy, entertainment, or something else?
- Can you classify the author's point of view (liberal, conservative, radical) and differentiate it from other points of view?
- What does the writer assume about the subject or about the audience? (What does unexplained jargon tell you?)
- How persuasive is the evidence? Which statements are facts, which inferences drawn from facts, and which matters of opinion? (See Chapter 14.)
- Are there relevant points you are aware of that the writer doesn't mention? What does this tell you?
- How compelling is the logic? Are there places where it doesn't make sense? How often?

Your answers to these questions should reveal the degree to which you accept the author's conclusions.

Cross-Reference Sources

Although at first it may seem daunting to answer all these questions, have patience and give the research process the time it needs. On a relatively new subject, the more you learn, the more you learn! The more differences you note, the more answers to the questions you find, and the more you know if a source might be useful.

21 b   Evaluating electronic sources

You need to apply the same critical scrutiny to Internet sources as to library sources, only more so. With no editor, librarian, or review board to screen for accuracy, reliability, or integrity, anyone with a computer and a modem can publish personal opinions, commercial pitches, bogus claims, bomb-making instructions, or smut on the Web. Although the Internet is a marvelous source of research information, it's also a trap for unwary researchers. So in addition to timeliness and perspective, what do you need to look out for? First, look at the electronic address (URL) to identify the type of organization sponsoring the site.

- ~ personal home page
- .aero aviation group
- .biz business
- .com commerce or business
- .coop credit union or rural co-op
- .edu educational institution
- .gov government institution
- .info information source open to the public
- .mil military institution
- .museum accredited museum
- .name second-level name
- .net news or other network
- .org nonprofit agency
- .pro professional organization

Each abbreviation suggests the potential bias in sites: .com and .biz sites are usually selling something; .coop and .pro may be selling something but may have a stronger interest in promoting the public welfare; .mil and .org are nonprofit, but each has an agenda to promote and defend; .edu, .gov, .museum, and .net should be less biased, but they still need careful checking; and .info, .name, or ~ could be anyone with any idea.

Second, ask as many critical questions as you would of a library source. An easy way to do this is to ask the reporter's questions (who, what, where, when, why, and how—see Chapter 11) and see what the answers tell you.

WHO IS THE SITE AUTHOR?

- Look for a person's name. Check the top or the bottom of the page.
- Look for credentials: scholar, scientist, doctor, college degrees, experience?
- If there is no personal name, look for a sponsoring organization. What does it stand for?
- Look for links to the author or agency's home page.
- Look for a way to contact the author or agency by e-mail, phone, or mail to ask further questions.

- If you cannot tell who created the site or contact its sponsors, site credibility is low. Don't rely on this site's information.

WHAT IDEAS OR INFORMATION DOES THE SITE PRESENT?

- Look for concepts and terminology you know.
- Look for facts versus inferences, opinions, and speculation. Be especially wary of opinion and speculation.
- Look for balanced versus biased points of view. What tips you off? Which would you trust more?
- Look for missing information. Why is it not there?
- Look for advertising. Is it openly identified and separated from factual material?

HOW IS THE INFORMATION PRESENTED?

- Look at the care with which the site is constructed, an indication of the education level of the author. If it contains spelling and grammar errors or is loaded with unexplained jargon, do you trust it? Will your readers?
- Look at the clarity of the graphics and/or sound features. Do they contribute to the content of the site?
- Look for links to other sites that suggest a connected, comprehensive knowledge base.

WHERE DOES THE INFORMATION COME FROM?

- Identify the source of the site: .edu, .gov, .com, and so on (see earlier).
- Identify the source of site facts. Do you trust it?
- Look for prior appearance as a print source. Are you familiar with it? Is it reputable?

WHEN WAS THE SITE CREATED?

- Look for the creation date or the date of latest update; a date more than a year old suggests a site that is not current.
- Look for absence of a creation date. Would lack of a date affect the reliability of the information?
- Look at whether or not the site is complete or still under construction. If incomplete, note that.

WHY IS THE INFORMATION PRESENTED?

- Look for clues to the agenda of the site. Is it to inform? Persuade? Entertain? Sell? Are you buying?
- Does getting information from the site cost money? (You should not have to pay for reference material for a college paper.)

Identify Anonymous Internet Sources

You can find out who owns a domain name—and often get contact addresses for owners or officers of a site—at the InterNIC WHOIS site run by Network Solutions Inc., the company responsible for administering most domain names: http://www.internic.net. But a site that makes you search for such information, rather than providing it for you, should not inspire confidence.

21 c Evaluating field sources

Unfortunately, the reliability and credibility of field sources is problematic because it is often more difficult for readers to track down field sources than textual sources. An interview is a onetime event, so a subject available one day may not be the next. A location providing information one day may change or become off limits the next. To examine field sources critically, you need to freeze them and make them hold still. Here's what to do.

Conduct Interviews

With the subject's permission, use a tape recorder and transcribe the whole session. Once an interview is taped, apply to it the critical questions you would a written source (see earlier). If you cannot tape-record, take careful notes, review main points with your subject before the interview ends, and apply these same critical questions.

Observe Sites

To freeze a site, make photographic or video records of what it looked like and what you found, in addition to taking copious notes about time, including details of location, size, shape, color, number, and so forth. If you cannot make photo records, sketch, draw, or diagram what you find. Pictures and careful verbal descriptions add credibility to papers by providing specific details that would be difficult to invent had the writer not been present. Even if you don't use them directly in your paper, visual notes will jog your memory of other important site events.

Control Personal Bias

Evaluating in-person observations is complicated because you are both the creator and the evaluator of the material. First, you shape interview material by the questions you ask, the manner in which you conduct the interview, and the language of your notes. Second, you shape on-site material by where you look, what you notice, and the language of your notes. In other words, in field research, the manner in which you collect and record information is most likely to introduce the most difficult bias to control, your own.

| **22** | *Using Research Sources* |

As you prepare to compose, assess all the information you've found and decide which sources to use and how. In other words, you need to synthesize unorganized raw material into an original, coherent paper.

To synthesize notes in preparation for writing, (1) look for connections among similar statements made by several sources, (2) look for contradictions between and among sources, and (3) marshal the evidence that furthers your paper's goal and set aside evidence that doesn't—everything you've collected cannot possibly fit and shouldn't.

Beware of constructing a source-driven paper, one whose direction is dictated by what you've found rather than what you are curious about and want to explore and examine. If you need more evidence, go get it rather than settling for answers to a question you haven't asked or faking it. Source-driven papers are obvious and odious to practiced instructors in every discipline.

Most research notes exist in three basic formats: direct quotation, paraphrase, and summary. Field notes may be more rambling. Whenever you quote, paraphrase, or summarize, be sure to document the source to the best of your ability.

22 a   Quotations

Direct quotations reproduce an author's or speaker's exact words. Direct quotations help you examine other people's ideas or add credibility to your own ideas. However, using too many quotations reduces your own authorial input, suggesting too much reliance on others' thoughts. Too many quotations can also be distracting; if you have more than two or three per page, it suggests that you haven't introduced, explained, or interpreted them well. In addition, long quotations slow readers down and invite skimming. Use only as much of a quotation as you need to support your point.

Using brief quotations gains space and readability. You can't change what a source says, but you can control how much of it you use. When you shorten a quotation, be careful not to change or distort its meaning. If you omit words within a quotation, indicate the missing words with ellipsis points (. . .) (see 66c). Any changes or additions must be indicated by including the new words in brackets.

ORIGINAL

The human communication environment has acquired biological complexity and planetary scale, but there are no scientists or activists monitoring it, theorizing about its health, or mounting campaigns to protect its resilience.

Stewart Brand, The Media Lab 258

INACCURATE QUOTATION (CHANGED MEANING)

In The Media Lab, Stewart Brand describes "biological complexity" as a hazard to scientists.

ACCURATE QUOTATION

In The Media Lab, Stewart Brand notes the growth and complexity of the modern telecommunications environment. But nobody is "monitoring it . . . to protect its resilience" (258).

Integrate Quotations into Your Paper

Integrate direct quotations smoothly into your paper by providing an explanatory tag at the beginning to explain the quote and show its relevance. Brief quotations (four or fewer typed lines) should be embedded in the main body of your paper and enclosed in quotation marks. The short quotation in the following passage is from a personal interview:

> Photo editor Tom Brennan took ten minutes to
> sort through my images and then told me, "Most
> photography editors wouldn't take more than two
> minutes to look at a portfolio."

Set off quotations of five lines or longer in block format, indented ten spaces (see Chapter 53, item 12).

Introduce Quotations

Introduce who is speaking, what the quotation refers to, and where it is from. If the author is well known, be sure to mention his or her name as part of the signal phrase.

> In <u>Walden</u>, Henry David Thoreau claims, "The mass
> of men lead lives of quiet desperation" (5).

If the title of your written work is well known, you can introduce a quotation with the title rather than the author's name, as long as the reference is clear.

> <u>Walden</u> sets forth one individual's antidote against
> the "lives of quiet desperation" led by the working
> class in mid-nineteenth-century America (Thoreau 5).

Use Signal Phrases

A signal phrase should accurately reflect the intention of the source. Unless the context requires a past-tense verb, use the present. To vary the verb in your signal phrase, consider synonyms such as *admits, argues, believes, claims, comments, finds, illustrates, observes, reports, reveals, says, speculates, suggests, wonders,* and *writes.*

Explain Quotations

Sometimes a quotation needs to be explained to ensure clarity, as in this final sentence:

> In <u>A Sand County Almanac</u>, Aldo Leopold invites
> urban readers to confront what they lose by living
> in the city: "There are two spiritual dangers in not
> owning a farm. One is the danger of supposing that
> breakfast comes from the grocery, and the other that
> heat comes from the furnace" (6). In other words,
> Leopold sees city dwellers as dangerously ignorant
> of how their basic needs are met.

You may also need to clarify what a word or reference means. Do this by using square brackets. In the following passage, it's unclear who will shrink.

UNCLEAR
Observing the remains of earwigs, sow bugs, moths, and spiders, Annie Dillard reminds us that everything is changing, even in death: "Next week, if the other bodies are any indication, he will be shrunken and gray, webbed to the floor with dust" (279).

CLEAR
Observing the remains of earwigs, sow bugs, moths, and spiders, Annie Dillard reminds us that everything is changing, even in death: "Next week, if the other bodies are any indication, [the earwig] will be shrunken and gray, webbed to the floor with dust" (279).

Adjust Grammar in Quoted Passages

A passage containing a quotation must follow all the rules of grammatical sentence structure—tenses should be consistent, verbs and subjects should agree, and so on. If the form of the passage doesn't fit the grammar of your own sentences, change your sentences, or slightly alter the quotation. Use this last option sparingly, and always indicate any changes with brackets.

GRAMMATICALLY INCOMPATIBLE
If Thoreau thought that in his day, "The mass of men lead lives of quiet desperation" (<u>Walden</u> 5), what would he say of the masses today?

GRAMMATICALLY COMPATIBLE
If Thoreau thought that in his day the masses led "lives of quiet desperation" (<u>Walden</u> 5), what would he say of the masses today?

GRAMMATICALLY COMPATIBLE
In the nineteenth century, Thoreau stated, "The mass of men lead lives of quiet desperation" (<u>Walden</u> 5). What would he say of the masses today?

GRAMMATICALLY COMPATIBLE
If Thoreau thought that in his day the "mass of men [led] lives of quiet desperation" (<u>Walden</u> 5), what would he say of the masses today?

- Quote directly when you cannot express the ideas better yourself.
- Quote directly when the original words are especially clear, powerful, or vivid.
- Quote directly when you want an authority's exact words to back you up.

22 b Paraphrasing

When you paraphrase, you restate an author's words in your own words to make the ideas clearer or to adapt them to your purpose. Paraphrases should generally re-create the original source's order, structure, and emphasis and include most details. A paraphrase should be clearer, but not necessarily briefer, than the original.

A paraphrase should neither distort meaning nor too closely follow the sentence patterns of the original (see Chapter 23). Follow these rules when you paraphrase:

- Check definitions of all words you don't know.
- Recast ideas in your own words.
- Don't paraphrase one sentence at a time—go for the meaning of the whole passage.
- Include any context necessary to explain the passage.

ORIGINAL
The human communication environment has acquired biological complexity and planetary scale, but there are no scientists or activists monitoring it, theorizing about its health, or mounting campaigns to protect its resilience.

Stewart Brand, <u>The Media Lab</u> 258

ACCURATE PARAPHRASE
Brand points out that our "communication environment" is as complex and vast as any

ecosystem on the planet, yet no one monitors this environment to keep track of its growth and warn us if something is about to go wrong (258).

22 c Summarizing

To summarize is to condense the main ideas of a passage into your own words. A summary includes only the essentials of the original, not the specific details. The length of the original source has no bearing on the length of your summary. You may summarize a paragraph, a chapter, or even a book in a few sentences. The more material summarized, however, the more general and abstract it becomes, so be careful not to distort the meaning of the original.

ORIGINAL
The human communication environment has acquired biological complexity and planetary scale, but there are no scientists or activists monitoring it, theorizing about its health, or mounting campaigns to protect its resilience.

Stewart Brand, The Media Lab 258

INACCURATE SUMMARY
The current telecommunications networks compose a nasty, unchangeable, and inescapable environment (Brand 258).

ACCURATE SUMMARY
Telecommunications networks have expanded so rapidly that monitoring and controlling them are difficult (Brand 258).

- Summarize to convey the main points of an original source but not the supporting details.
- Summarize to provide an overview or an interesting aside without digressing from your paper's focus.
- Summarize to condense lengthy notes into tight sentences.

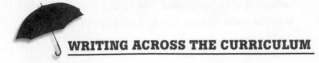

WRITING ACROSS THE CURRICULUM

Using Visual Images

Visual images enhance papers, portfolios, and Web pages in many disciplines across the curriculum. Images inform, entertain, and engage readers in ways text alone does not by breaking up dense textual space, by signaling a shift in ideas or information, or by adding pertinent information. The following examples illustrate some possibilities:

- Use images that save you a thousand words. For example, many of the images that illustrate Chapter 6 in this handbook are especially rich in visual information.

- Use images that convey useful information quickly in the shorthand way of charts and graphs, as does this Regional Sales Distribution chart below.

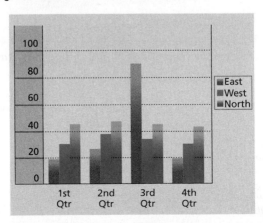

- Use images that make abstract ideas concrete. It would take a lot of words and a long time to describe a cartoon character such as a Smurf to somebody who had never seen the television show.

- Control the size and layout of images using a computer program such as MS Paint or Adobe Photoshop or judicious cutting and pasting with scissors and tape.

- Position images where they belong—or as near as possible—in your text.

- Explain or refer to images that convey content information in your text.

- Label each image appropriately, following conventions such as MLA style in formal papers (Figure 1: Roadside Stand Near Birmingham, AL, by Walker Evans) or more casually, as we did with captions in Chapter 3.

- If publishing on a Web site, make sure the image is in the public domain (as is the Walker Evans photograph, above) or secure permission from the copyright holder.

23 | Avoiding Plagiarism

The rule is simple: When, in writing a paper, you use other people's ideas or language, you must give credit to the authors whose ideas and words you have used. If you don't, you have stolen their ideas or words and are guilty of plagiarism. In Western culture, plagiarism is a serious offense, one that has cost writers, reporters, artists, musicians, and scientists their reputations, jobs, and vast sums of money. Plagiarism is especially serious within academic communities, where the generation of original research, ideas, and words is the central mission of the institution.

The Internet has made the copying of research sources especially easy, which saves researchers an enormous amount of time. However, Internet copying has also made plagiarism easy. To avoid plagiarizing, you need to know exactly what plagiarism is and how to avoid committing it.

23 a   What plagiarism *is*

Plagiarism is putting one's name on a paper written by a friend and turning it in. It's buying a term paper from a term-paper factory and pretending that you have written it. It's downloading a report from the Internet and substituting your name for the original author's name. In any of these flagrant examples, the intent to plagiarize is deliberate and obvious, something that serious and honorable students would never do.

However, plagiarism also occurs when well-meaning students get lazy, careless, or pressured in their note-taking, composing, or documenting. Here are three examples of unintentional plagiarism: (1) A student copies a passage word-for-word from an Internet site and pastes it word-for-word into a paper, but without quotation marks or author attribution. (2) A student summarizes, but does not directly quote, a published author's idea and omits both the author's name and the book's title. (3) A student credits an author's idea in a signal phrase ("According to . . .") but omits quotation marks around the author's exact phrases. None of these may be intentional, but each is an act of plagiarism, and each could be avoided by clearer knowledge and more careful research practice.

23 b   What plagiarism is *not*

Writers don't need to attribute everything they write or say to specific sources. For example, what we call common knowledge does not need documentation. You do not need to credit common historical, cultural, or geographical information that an educated American adult can be expected to know. Nor do you need to attribute to specific authorities the factual information that appears in multiple sources, such as the dates of historical events (the sack of Rome in AD 410, the adoption of the Declaration of Independence on July 4, 1776), the names and locations of states and cities, the general laws of science (gravity, motion), or statements of well-known theories (feminism, supply and demand, evolution).

You don't need to document current knowledge in widespread use in your own culture (global warming, cloning, urban sprawl). Nor do you need to document what is well known in the field in which you are writing or the most basic information that can be found in textbooks and lectures. For example, you need not document the terms "libido" or "superego" (associated with Sigmund Freud) in a psychology paper or "myth" or "postmodern" in an English, history, art, or philosophy paper. In other words, within a given interpretive community, basic ideas and knowledge can be assumed to be the common property of all members of that community. However, specific positions or interpretations within a community do need to be specifically identified.

23 c Recognizing and avoiding plagiarism

Intentional plagiarism is simply cheating, which honest students avoid. Unintentional plagiarism, a far more common problem, occurs when a writer paraphrases or summarizes another author but stays too close to the wording or sentence structure of the original. The following examples will help you avoid unintentional plagiarism. This first example shows the student writing a paper on Machievelli's *The Prince,* where he is citing a scholarly text:

ORIGINAL
Notwithstanding the widely different opinions about Machiavelli's work and his personality, there is at least one point in which we find a complete unanimity. All authors emphasize that Machiavelli is a child of his age, that he is a typical witness to the Renaissance.

—Ernst Cassirer, The Myth of the State

PLAGIARIZED PARAPHRASE
Despite the widely different opinions about Machiavelli's work and his personality, everyone agrees that he is a representative witness to the Renaissance (Cassirer 43).

Even though Cassirer is credited with the idea, the writer does not credit him with the specific wording, which the writer has copied almost word-for-word.

ACCEPTABLE PARAPHRASE
Although views on the work and personality of
Machiavelli vary, everyone agrees that he was "a
typical witness to the Renaissance" (Cassirer 43).

In this second example, from a popular culture source,
the student is writing a paper for a film professor about
comic book heroes portrayed in the movies. She decides to
use this passage in Roger Ebert's review of *Spider-Man* for
the *Chicago Sun-Times* (May 3, 2002):

> Remember the first time you saw the characters
> defy gravity in <u>Crouching Tiger, Hidden Dragon</u>?
> They transcended gravity, but they didn't dismiss
> it: They seemed to possess weight, dimension
> and presence. Spider-Man as he leaps across the
> rooftops is landing too lightly, rebounding too much
> like a bouncing ball. He looks like a video game
> figure, not like a person having an amazing
> experience.

Ebert's whole review is readily available on the Internet, easily accessed via the Internet Movie Database
(http://www.imdb.com/), so that it's especially easy to block
and copy parts to paste directly into the paper you are writing instead of onto a note card for further study. (In an academic paper, the citation would appear on a "Works Cited"
[MLA] or "References" [APA, CMS] page; if academic style
is not required, including author and title in a signal phrase
would give proper credit.) If the research writer does not
follow proper citation guidelines, he or she might inadver-
tently plagiarize, as the following examples illustrate.

- It is plagiarism if the student cut and pasted the Spider-
  Man passage above directly into the paper without
  acknowledging that it was written by Roger Ebert.

  - To fix, credit in a signal phrase (According to Roger
    Ebert . . .), put the passage in quotation marks, and
    in an academic paper, identify where the passage
    came from and when it was published on a "Works
    Cited" page (MLA), "References" page (APA), or foot-
    note (CMS) page as appropriate (see Chapters 29,
    34, and 38).

- It is plagiarism if the student wrote:

    > The problem with Spider-Man is the video-game quality of the characters who bound from roof to roof and don't seem to be affected by gravity— unlike the more realistic figures in the movie Crouching Tiger, Hidden Dragon.

    - In this case the student lifts Ebert's idea in clearly identifiable ways but does not quote Ebert directly. To fix, credit in a signal phrase (Roger Ebert claims the problem with Spider-Man is the video-game quality . . .) and, if an academic paper, identify where the passage came from and when it was published in the appropriate academic convention.

- It is plagiarism if the student lifted key portions of Ebert's exact language from the passage without using quotation marks:

    > Roger Ebert claims that the characters in Crouching Tiger, Hidden Dragon transcended gravity, but they didn't dismiss it.

    - Though Ebert is credited with the idea, he is not credited with the specific language. To fix, put quotation marks around the words borrowed: Roger Ebert claims that the characters in *Crouching Tiger, Hidden Dragon* "transcended gravity, but they didn't dismiss it." Again, if this is an academic paper, identify where the passage came from and when it was published on the appropriate reference page.

WRITING ACROSS THE CURRICULUM

Guidelines for Avoiding Plagiarism

Plagiarism is a serious offense in every field and department across the curriculum. In simplest terms, it's the act of copying somebody else's work and passing it off as your own. In addition to the many obvious cases described in this chapter, it's plagiarism to copy the results of a neighbor's biology experiment in your lab report; to copy a chart or graph from an economics textbook without credit; and to hand in somebody else's field notes as your own. Below are simple guidelines for avoiding plagiarism:

- For all copied sources, note who said what, where, and when.
- When using quoted material, do not distort or intentionally modify an author's meaning.
- Print out and save at least the first page of all online material, making sure it contains the Internet address and date.
- Hand copy identifying information (name, title, date, place of publication) on all photocopied or printed source pages.
- Place all exactly copied language in quotation marks.
- In writing a paraphrase or summary, credit the author and recast the original material into your own language.
- Identify all borrowed ideas and language with appropriate references using the appropriate documentation system (MLA, APA, CMS, etc.).

24 | *Writing in the Disciplines*

Good writing satisfies the expectations of an audience in form, style, and content. But different audiences come to a piece of writing with different expectations, so writing that is judged "good" by one audience may be judged "less good" by another. Although all college instructors value good writing, each area of study has its own set of criteria by which writing is judged. For instance, an informal, conversational style that might please a humanities instructor may be frowned upon by a social science instructor. This chapter provides a broad outline of the different expectations you might encounter from discipline to discipline.

24 a   Differences among disciplines

As a rule, knowledge in the humanities focuses on texts and on individual ideas, speculations, insights, and imaginative connections. Interpretation in the humanities is thus relatively subjective. Accordingly, good writing in the humanities is characterized by personal involvement, lively language, and speculative or open-ended conclusions.

In contrast, knowledge in the social and physical sciences is likely to focus on data and on ideas that can be verified through observing, measuring, and testing. Interpretation in these disciplines needs to be objective.

Accordingly, good writing in the social and physical sciences emphasizes inferences based on the careful study of data and downplays the personal opinion and speculation of the writer.

But boundaries between the disciplines are not absolute. For example, at some colleges history is considered one of the humanities, while at others it is classified as a social science. Geography is a social science when it looks at regions and how people live, but it is a physical science when it investigates the properties of rocks and glaciers. Colleges of business, engineering, health, education, and natural resources all draw on numerous disciplines as their sources of knowledge.

The field of English alone includes not only the study of literature but also literary theory and history, not only composition but also creative and technical writing. In addition, English departments often include linguistics, journalism, folklore, women's studies, African American studies, and sometimes speech, film, and communications. In other words, within even one discipline, you might be asked to write several distinct types of papers: personal experience essays for a composition course, interpretations for a literature course, abstracts for a linguistics course, short stories for a creative writing course. Consequently, any observations about the different kinds of knowledge and the differing conventions for writing about them are only generalizations. The more carefully you study any one discipline, the more complex it becomes, and the harder it is to make a generalization that doesn't have numerous exceptions.

Formal differences exist among the styles of writing for different disciplines, especially in the conventions for documenting sources. Each discipline has its own authority or authorities, which provide rules about such issues as spelling of technical terms and preferred punctuation and editing mechanics, as well as documentation style. In addition, if you write for publication in a magazine, professional journal, or book, the publisher will have a *house style,* which may vary in some details from the conventions listed in the authoritative guidelines for the discipline in which you are writing.

24 b Similarities among disciplines

Regardless of disciplinary differences, certain principles of good writing hold true *across* the curriculum.

Knowledge

Each field of study attempts to develop knowledge about a particular aspect of the physical, social, or cultural world in which we live. For example, the physical sciences observe nature to learn how it works, whereas history and anthropology examine civilizations over time, sociology looks at human beings in groups, and psychology attempts to explain the operation and development of the individual human mind. In writing for a particular course, keep in mind the larger purpose of the field of study, especially when selecting, introducing, and concluding your investigation.

Method

Each field has accepted methods of investigation. Perhaps the best known is the scientific method, used in most of the physical and social sciences. One who uses the scientific method first asks a question, then poses a possible answer (a hypothesis), then carries out experiments in field or laboratory to test this answer, and finally, if it cannot be disproved, concludes that the hypothesis is correct. However, while research in the social sciences follows this scientific pattern, some disciplines, such as anthropology, rely instead on the more personal approach of ethnographic study. Literary research may be formal, historical, deconstructive, and so on. It is important to recognize that every discipline has its accepted—and its controversial—methods of study. Any conclusions you discuss in your writing should reflect that awareness.

Evidence

In every field, any claim you make about the subject of your study needs to be supported by evidence. If, in order to identify an unknown rock, you scrape it with a known rock in the geology laboratory, the scratch marks of the harder rock on the softer rock will be part of your evidence to support your claims about the unknown rock. If you analyze Holden Caulfield on the basis of his opening monologue in *The Catcher in the Rye,* his words will be evidence to support your interpretation. If you conduct a survey of students to examine college study habits, counting and collating your findings will be evidence to support your conclusions. In other words, although the *nature* of evidence varies greatly from one discipline to another, the *need* for evidence is constant. In some cases, when you need to support an assertion, you will consult certain sources for evidence and will need to have clear documentation for these sources. (Chapters 24–38 provide detailed guidelines for documenting sources in various disciplines.)

Accuracy

Each field values precision and correctness, and each has its own specialized vocabulary for talking about knowledge. Writers are expected to use terms precisely and to spell them correctly. In addition, each discipline has developed formats in which to report information. When you write within a discipline, you should know the correct form in which to communicate a literary analysis in English, a research report in sociology, or a laboratory report in biology. Each discipline also values conventional correctness in language. Your writing will be most respected when it reflects standard use of grammar, punctuation, and mechanics.

MLA MLA MLA MLA MLA

25 | Guidelines for MLA Manuscripts

The most common and most economical form for documenting sources in research-based English papers is the MLA (Modern Language Association) system, described here.

- All sources are briefly mentioned by author name in the text.
- A list of Works Cited at the end lists full publication data for each source named in the paper.
- Additional explanatory information written by the writer of the paper can be included in footnotes or endnotes.

The MLA documentation system is explained in authoritative detail in the *MLA Handbook for Writers of Research Papers,* 6th edition (New York: MLA, 2003), or on the MLA Web site http://www.mla.org.

The MLA guidelines for submitting college papers are fairly conservative and do not reflect the wealth of visually interesting options in fonts, point sizes, visual insertions, and other features available on most modern word processors. If your instructor requests MLA format, follow the guidelines here. If your instructor encourages more open journalistic formats, use good judgment in displaying the information in your text.

Paper and Printing

Print all academic assignments on clean white 8½-by-11-inch paper in a standard font (e.g., Times New Roman, Courier) and point size (11–12) using a good-quality printer.

Margins and Spacing

Allow margins of one inch all around. Justify the left margin only. Double-space everything, including headings, quoted material, and the Works Cited page. Indent the first line of each paragraph five spaces or one-half inch. Indent every line of a prose quotation of more than four lines or poetry of more than three lines twice as far—ten spaces or one inch. (Do not use quotation marks when quotations are displayed in this way.)

Identification

On page 1, include your name, instructor's name, course title, and the date on separate lines, double-spaced, flush with the upper left margin. Double-space to the title.

Title

Center the title on the first page using conventional title case punctuation (capitalizing key words only). If your instructor asks for strict MLA style, avoid using italics, underlining, quotation marks, boldface, unusual fonts, or an enlarged point size for the title. (MLA does not require a title page or an outline.) Double-space to the first paragraph.

Page Numbers

Set page numbers to print in the upper right margin of all pages, one-half inch below the top of the paper. If following strict MLA form, include your last name before each page number to guarantee correct identification of stray pages (Turner 1, Turner 2, etc.).

Punctuation

Use one space after commas, semicolons, colons, periods, question marks, exclamation points, and between the periods in an ellipsis. Dashes are formed by two hyphens, with no extra spacing on either side.

Visual Information

Label each table or chart as Table 1, Table 2, and so on. Label each drawing or photograph as Figure 1 (or Fig. 1), Figure 2, and so on. Include a clear caption for each, and place it in the text as near as possible to the passage that refers to it.

26 | *Guidelines for In-Text Citations*

The following guidelines explain how to include research sources in the main body of your text using MLA style.

26 a Citing sources in the text

Each source mentioned in your paper needs to be accompanied by a brief citation consisting of the author's last name and the page number. These are placed either in the text itself or in parentheses following the cited material. This **in-text citation** refers readers to the alphabetical list of Works Cited at the paper's end, which gives full publication information about each source.

1. Author identified in a signal phrase

When you include the source author's name in the sentence introducing the source, add only the specific page on which the material appeared in parentheses following the information.

> Carol Lea Clark explains the basic necessities for the creation of a page on the World Wide Web (77).

Do not include the word *page* or the abbreviation *p.* before the number; the parenthetical reference comes before the period.

For a work by *two or three authors,* include all authors' names:

> Clark and Jones explain . . .

For works with *more than three authors,* list all authors or use the first author's name and add *et al.* (Latin abbreviation for "and others") without a comma:

> Britton et al. suggest . . .

2. Author not identified in a signal phrase

If you do not mention the author's name in your text, add it in the parentheses just before the source page number. Do not punctuate between the author's name and the page number.

> Provided one has certain "basic ingredients," the
> Web offers potential worldwide publication
> (Clark 77).

For a work by two or three authors, include all authors' last names:

> (Clark and Jones 15)
>
> (Smith, Web, and Beck 210).

For works with more than three authors, list all authors' last names or list the first author only, adding *et al.*

> (White et al. 95)

3. Two or more works by the same author

Each citation needs to identify the specific work. If there are two or more works by the same author on your Works Cited list, you must indicate which work is being cited. Either mention the title of the work in the text, or include a shortened version of the title (usually the first one or two important words) in the parenthetical citation. Here are three correct ways to do this:

> According to Lewis Thomas in *Lives of a Cell*, many
> bacteria become dangerous only if they
> manufacture exotoxins (76).
>
> According to Lewis Thomas, many bacteria become
> dangerous only if they manufacture exotoxins
> (*Lives* 76).
>
> Many bacteria become dangerous only if they
> manufacture exotoxins (Thomas, *Lives* 76).

Identify the shortened title by underlining (e.g., published titles) or quotation marks (e.g., articles), as appropriate.

4. Unknown author

When the author of a work is unknown, either give the complete title in the text or a shortened version in the parenthetical citation, along with the page number.

> According to *Statistical Abstracts*, in 1990 the
> literacy rate for Mexico stood at 75% (374).
>
> In 1990 the literacy rate for Mexico stood at 75%
> (*Statistical* 374).

5. Corporate or organizational author

Indicate the group's full name in either text or parentheses:

> (Florida League of Women Voters 3)

If the name is long, it is best to cite it in the text sentence and put only the page number in parentheses.

6. Authors with the same last name

When you cite works by two or more different authors with the same last name, include the first initial of each author's name in the parenthetical citation:

> (C. Miller 63; S. Miller 101–04).

7. Works in more than one volume

Indicate the pertinent volume number for each citation before the page number, and follow it with a colon and one space:

> (Hill 2: 70)

If your source is one volume of a multivolume work, do not specify the volume number in your text, but specify it in the Works Cited list.

8. One-page works

When you refer to a work that is one page long, do not include the page number because it will appear in the Works Cited list.

9. Quotation from a secondary source

When a quotation or any information in your source is originally from another source, use the abbreviation *qtd. in.*

> Lester Brown of Worldwatch feels that
> international agricultural production has
> reached its limit (qtd. in Mann 51).

10. Poem or play

In citing poems, name part (if divided into parts) and line numbers; include the word *line* or *lines* in the first such reference.

> In "The Mother," Gwendolyn Brooks remembers
> "the children you got that you did not get" (line 1).

MLA MLA MLA

When you cite up to three lines from a poem in your text, separate the lines with a slash, with a space before and after it.

> Emily Dickinson describes being alive in a New England summer: "Inebriate of air am I / And debauchee of dew / Reeling through endless summer days" (lines 6–8).

When you cite more than three lines, indent each line ten spaces or one inch (see item 12).

Cite plays using act, scene, and (for verse plays) line numbers, separated by periods. For major works such as *Hamlet,* use identifiable abbreviations.

> (Ibsen 2.2)   (<u>Ham</u>. 4.4.31.39)

11. More than one work in a citation

To cite two or more works, separate them with semicolons.

> (Aronson, *Golden Shore* 177; Didion 49–50)

12. Long quotation set off from text

To set off quoted passages of five or more lines, indent ten spaces or one inch from the left-hand margin of the text (not from the paper's edge), double-space, and omit quotation marks. The parenthetical citation *follows* end punctuation (unlike citations for shorter, integrated quotations) and is not followed by a period.

> Fellow author W. Somerset Maugham had this to say about Austen's dialogue:
>
>> No one has ever looked upon Jane Austen as a great stylist. Her spelling was peculiar and her grammar often shaky, but she had a good ear. Her dialogue is probably as natural as dialogue can ever be. To set down on paper speech as it is spoken would be very tedious, and some arrangement of it is necessary. (434)

13. Electronic texts

The MLA guidelines on documenting electronic sources are explained in detail online at http://www.mla.org/set_stl.htm.

Electronic sources are cited in the body of the text the same as print sources: by author, title of text or title of Web site, and page numbers. If no page numbers appear on the source, include section (sec.) number or title, and/or paragraph (par.) numbers.

> The Wizard of Oz "was nominated for six
> Academy Awards, including Best Picture"
> (Wizard par. 3).

However, Web pages commonly omit page and section numbers and are not organized by paragraphs. In such cases, omit numbers from your parenthetical references. (For a document downloaded from the Web, the page numbers of a printout should normally not be cited because pagination may vary in different printouts.)

> In the United States, the birth rate per 1,000
> people has fallen steadily from 16.7 in 1995
> to 12.1 in 2004 (Statistical).

26 b Using notes to provide more information

MLA style uses notes primarily to offer comments, explanations, or additional information (especially source-related information) that cannot be smoothly or easily accommodated in the text of the paper. In general, however, avoid presenting information outside the main body of your paper, unless it is necessary for clarification or justification. If a note is necessary, insert a raised (superscript) numeral at the reference point in the text. Introduce the note itself with a corresponding raised numeral, and indent it.

TEXT WITH SUPERSCRIPT

The standard ingredients for guacamole include avocados, lemon juice, onion, tomatoes, coriander, salt, and pepper.[1] Hurtado's poem, however, gives this traditional dish a whole new twist (lines 10–17).

NOTE

[1]For variations, see Beard 314, Egerton 197, and Eckhardt 92. Beard's version, which includes olives and green peppers, is the most unusual.

Any published references listed in the notes must also appear in the Works Cited list.

Notes may come at the bottom of the page on which the superscript appears, single-spaced, as footnotes, or they may be presented as endnotes, double-spaced, on a separate page at the end of your paper, preceding the Works Cited list, with the title "Note" or "Notes."

27 | *Sample First Page in MLA Style*

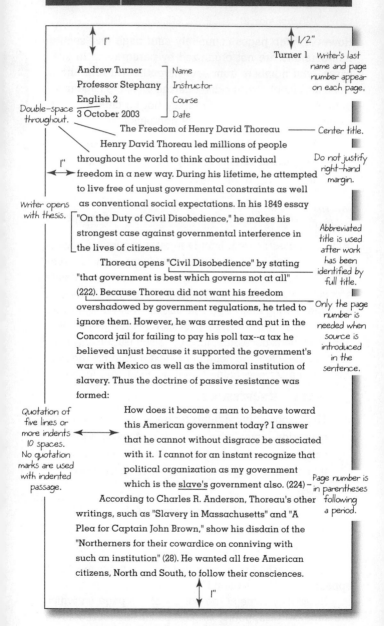

1"

1/2"

Turner 1   *Writer's last name and page number appear on each page.*

Andrew Turner   *Name*

Professor Stephany   *Instructor*

English 2   *Course*

Double-space throughout.   3 October 2003   *Date*

       The Freedom of Henry David Thoreau ——— *Center title.*

       Henry David Thoreau led millions of people

1"   throughout the world to think about individual

freedom in a new way. During his lifetime, he attempted   *Do not justify right-hand margin.*

to live free of unjust governmental constraints as well

Writer opens with thesis.   as conventional social expectations. In his 1849 essay

"On the Duty of Civil Disobedience," he makes his

strongest case against governmental interference in

the lives of citizens.

       Thoreau opens "Civil Disobedience" by stating   *Abbreviated title is used after work has been identified by full title.*

"that government is best which governs not at all"

(222). Because Thoreau did not want his freedom

overshadowed by government regulations, he tried to   *Only the page number is needed when source is introduced in the sentence.*

ignore them. However, he was arrested and put in the

Concord jail for failing to pay his poll tax--a tax he

believed unjust because it supported the government's

war with Mexico as well as the immoral institution of

slavery. Thus the doctrine of passive resistance was

formed:

Quotation of five lines or more indents 10 spaces. No quotation marks are used with indented passage.

           How does it become a man to behave toward

           this American government today? I answer

           that he cannot without disgrace be associated

           with it. I cannot for an instant recognize that

           political organization as my government

           which is the <u>slave's</u> government also. (224) –   *Page number is in parentheses following a period.*

According to Charles R. Anderson, Thoreau's other

writings, such as "Slavery in Massachusetts" and "A

Plea for Captain John Brown," show his disdain of the

"Northerners for their cowardice on conniving with

such an institution" (28). He wanted all free American

citizens, North and South, to follow their consciences.

1"

Sample First Page of a Student Essay in MLA Format

28 | *Guidelines for the MLA Works Cited Page*

I dentify every source mentioned in the body of your paper in a Works Cited list attached to the end of the paper using the following format.

- Center the title Works Cited, with no quotation marks, underlining, or boldface, one inch from the top of a separate page following the final page of the paper.

- Number this page, following in sequence from the last numbered page of your paper. If the list runs more than a page, continue the page numbering in sequence, but do not repeat the Works Cited title.

- Double-space between the title and first entry and within and between entries.

- Begin each entry at the left-hand margin, and indent subsequent lines the equivalent of a paragraph indention (five spaces or one-half inch).

28 a   Documenting Books

1. Book by one author

> Thomas, Lewis. <u>Lives of a Cell: Notes of a Biology Watcher</u>. New York: Viking, 1974.

2. Book by two or three authors

> Fulwiler, Toby, and Alan R. Hayakawa. <u>The Blair Handbook</u>, 5th ed. Upper Saddle River: Prentice, 2007.

Second and third authors are listed first name first. Do not alphabetize the authors' names within an individual Works Cited entry. The final author's name is preceded by *and;* do not use an ampersand (*&*). A comma always follows the inverted ordering of the author's first name.

3. Book by more than three authors

> Britton, James, et al. <u>The Development of Writing Abilities 11-18</u>. London: Macmillan, 1975.

With more than three authors, you have the option of using the abbreviation *et al.* (Latin for "and others") or listing all the authors' names in full as they appear on the title page of the book. Do not alphabetize the names within the Works Cited entry.

4. Book by a corporation, organization, or association

> U.S. Coast Guard Auxiliary. <u>Boating Skills and
> Seamanship</u>. Washington: Coast Guard
> Auxiliary National Board, 1997.

Alphabetize by the name of the organization.

5. Revised edition of a book

> Hayakawa, S. I. <u>Language in Thought and Action</u>.
> 4th ed. New York: Harcourt, 1978.

6. Edited book

> Hoy, Pat C., II, Esther H. Schor, and Robert DiYanni,
> eds. <u>Women's Voices: Visions and
> Perspectives</u>. New York: McGraw, 1990.

7. Book with an editor and author

> Britton, James. <u>Prospect and Retrospect</u>. Ed. Gordon
> Pradl. Upper Montclair: Boynton, 1982.

The abbreviation *Ed.* when followed by a name replaces the phrase *Edited by* and cannot be made plural. (See models 13 and 14.)

8. Book in more than one volume

> Waldrep, Tom, ed. <u>Writers on Writing</u>. 2 vols. New
> York: Random, 1985-88.

When separate volumes were published in different years, use inclusive dates.

9. One volume of a multivolume book

> Waldrep, Tom, ed. <u>Writers on Writing</u>, Vol. 2. New
> York: Random, 1988.

When each volume has its own title, list the full publication information for the volume first, followed by information on the series (number of volumes, dates).

Churchill, Winston S. <u>Triumph and Tragedy</u>. Boston: Houghton, 1953. Vol. 6 of <u>The Second World War</u>. 6 vols. 1948-53.

10. Translated book

Camus, Albert. <u>The Stranger</u>. Trans. Stuart Gilbert. New York: Random, 1946.

11. Book in a series

Magistrate, Anthony. <u>Stephen King, The Second Decade</u>: Danse Macabre <u>to</u> The Dark Half. Twayne American Authors Series 599. New York: Twayne, 1992.

A book title appearing within another book's title is not underlined. Add series information just before the city of publication.

12. Reprinted book

Hurston, Zora Neale. <u>Their Eyes Were Watching God</u>. 1937. New York: Perennial-Harper, 1990.

Add the original publication date after the title; then cite information for the current edition.

13. Introduction, preface, foreword, or afterword in a book

Selfe, Cynthia. Foreword. <u>Electronic Communication Across the Curriculum</u>. Ed. Donna Rice et al. Urbana: NCTE, 1998. ix-xiv.

14. Work in an anthology or chapter in an edited collection

Donne, John. "The Canonization." <u>The Metaphysical Poets</u>. Ed. Helen Gardner. Baltimore: Penguin, 1957. 61-62.

Use quotation marks around the title of a poem, a short story, an essay, or a chapter. For a work originally published as a book, underline the title. Add inclusive page numbers. When citing two or more selections from one anthology, list the anthology separately under the editor's name. All entries within that anthology will then include only a cross-reference to the anthology entry.

Donne, John. "The Canonization." Gardner 61-62.

15. Essay or periodical article reprinted in a collection

> Emig, Janet. "Writing as Mode of Learning." <u>College Composition and Communication</u> 28 (1977): 122-28. Rpt. in <u>The Web of Meaning</u>. Ed. Janet Emig. Upper Montclair: Boynton, 1983. 123-31.

> Gannet, Lewis. Introduction. <u>The Portable Steinbeck</u>. New York: Viking, 1946. 1-12. Rpt. as "John Steinbeck's Way of Writing" in <u>Steinbeck and His Critics: A Record of Twenty-five Years</u>. Ed. E. W. Tedlock, Jr., and C. V. Wicker. Albuquerque: U of New Mexico P, 1957. 23-37.

Include the full citation for the original publication, followed by *Rpt. in* ("Reprinted in") and the publication information for the book. Add inclusive page numbers for the article or essay found in the collection; add inclusive page numbers for the original source when available.

16. Article in a reference book

> "Behn, Aphra." <u>The Concise Columbia Encyclopedia</u>. 1998 ed.

> Miller, Peter L. "The Power of Flight." <u>The Encyclopedia of Insects</u>. Ed. Christopher O'Toole. New York: Facts on File, 1986. 18-19.

For a signed article, begin with the author's name. For commonly known reference works, full publication information and editors' names are not necessary. For entries arranged alphabetically, page and volume numbers are not necessary.

17. Anonymous book

> <u>The World Almanac and Book of Facts</u>. New York: World Almanac-Funk, 2000.

Alphabetize by title, excluding an initial *A, An,* or *The.*

> <u>Holy Bible. King James Text: Modern Phrased Version</u>. New York: Oxford UP, 1980.

18. Government document

> United States. Central Intelligence Agency. <u>National
>   Basic Intelligence Fact Book</u>. Washington:
>   GPO, 1999.

If the author is identified, begin with that name. If not, begin with the government (country or state), followed by the agency or organization. The U.S. Government Printing Office is abbreviated *GPO*.

19. Dissertation, unpublished or published

> Kitzhaber, Albert R. "Rhetoric in American
>   Colleges." Diss. U of Washington, 1953.

Use quotation marks for the title of an unpublished dissertation. Include the university name and the year. For a published dissertation, underline the title and give publication information as you would for a book, including the order number if the publisher is University Microfilms International (UMI).

28 b Documenting periodicals

20. Article, story, or poem in a monthly or bimonthly magazine

> Linn, Robert A., and Stephen B. Dunbar. "The
>   Nation's Report Card Goes Home." <u>Phi Delta
>   Kappan</u> Jan. 2000: 127-43.

Abbreviate all months except May, June, and July. Hyphenate months for bimonthlies (*July–Aug. 1993*). Do not list volume or issue numbers. If the article is unsigned, alphabetize by title.

21. Article, story, or poem in a weekly magazine

> Ross, Alex. "The Wanderer." <u>New Yorker</u> 10 May
>   1999: 56-53.

Note that when the day of the week is specified, the publication date is inverted.

22. Article in a daily newspaper

> Brody, Jane E. "Doctors Get Poor Marks for Nutrition
>   Knowledge." <u>New York Times</u> 10 Feb. 1992: B7.

"Redistricting Reconsidered." <u>Washington Post</u> 12
    May 1999: B2.

For an unsigned article, alphabetize by the title. Give the
full name of the newspaper as it appears on the masthead,
but drop any introductory *A, An,* or *The.* If the city is not
in the name, it should follow in brackets: *El Diario [Los
Angeles].*

23. Article in a journal paginated by volume

Harris, Joseph. "The Other Reader." <u>Journal of
    Advanced Composition</u> 12 (1992): 34-36.

If the page numbers are continuous from one issue to the
next throughout the year, include only the volume number
(in Arabic numerals) and year. Do not give the issue number or the month or season.

24. Article in a journal paginated by issue

Tiffin, Helen. "Post-Colonialism, Post-Modernism,
    and the Rehabilitation of Post-Colonial
    History." <u>Journal of Commonwealth Literature</u>
    23.1 (1998): 169-81.

If each issue begins with page 1, include the volume number followed by a period and then the issue number (both
in Arabic numerals, even if the journal uses Roman).

25. Editorial

"Gay Partnership Legislation a Mixed Bag."
    Editorial. <u>Burlington Free Press</u> 5 April 2000:
    A10.

If the editorial is signed, list the author's name first.

26. Letter to the editor and reply

Kempthorne, Charles. Letter. <u>Kansas City Star</u> 26
    July 1999: A16.

27. Review

Kramer, Mimi. "Victims" Rev. of <u>'Tis Pity She's a
    Whore</u>. New York Shakespeare Festival. <u>New
    Yorker</u> 20 Apr. 1992: 78-79.

28 c Databases

The Works Cited entries for electronic databases (newsletters, journals, and conferences) are similar to entries for articles in printed periodicals. Portable databases are much like books and periodicals. Their entries in Works Cited lists are similar to those for printed material except that you must also include the following items.

■ The medium of publication (*CD-ROM, diskette, magnetic tape*).

■ The name of the vendor, if known. (This may be different from the name of the organization that compiled the information, which must also be included.)

■ The date of electronic publication, in addition to the date the material originally may have been published (as for a reprinted book or article).

28. Periodically updated CD-ROM database

> James, Caryn. "An Army as Strong as Its Weakest Link." New York Times 16 Sep. 1994: C8. New York Times Ondisc. CD-ROM. UMI-Proquest. Oct. 1994.

If a database comes from a printed source such as a book, periodical, or collection of bibliographies or abstracts, cite this information first, followed by the title of the database (underlined), the medium of publication, the vendor name (if applicable), and the date of electronic publication. If no printed source is available, include the title of the material accessed (in quotation marks), the date of the material if given, the underlined title of the database, the medium of publication, the vendor name, and the date of electronic publication.

29. Nonperiodical CD-ROM publication

> "Rhetoric." The Oxford English Dictionary. 2nd ed. CD-ROM. Oxford: Oxford UP, 1992.

List a nonperiodical CD-ROM as you would a book, adding the medium of publication and information about the source, if applicable. If citing only part of a work, underline the title of the selected portion or place it within quotation marks, as appropriate (as you would the title of a printed short story, poem, article, essay, or similar source).

30. Diskette or magnetic tape publication

Doyle, Roddy. <u>The Woman Who Walked into Doors</u>.
　　　Magnetic tape. New York: Penguin
　　　Audiobooks, 1996.

List these in the Works Cited section as you would a book, adding the medium of publication (for example, *Diskette* or *Magnetic tape*).

28 d Documenting electronic sources

Online Sources

Documenting a World Wide Web (WWW) or other Internet source follows the same basic guidelines as documenting other texts: cite *who* said *what, where,* and *when.* However, important differences need to be noted. In citing online sources from the World Wide Web or electronic mail, two dates are important: the date the text was created (published) and the date you found the information (accessed the site). When both publication and access dates are available, provide both.

　　Many WWW sources are often updated or changed, leaving no trace of the original version, so always provide the access date, which documents that this information was available on that particular date. Thus, most electronic source entries will end with an access date immediately followed by the electronic address: 23 Dec. 2003 <http://www.cas.usf.edu/english>. The angle brackets < > identify the source as the Internet.

31. Work from an online database

Conniff, Richard. "Approaching Walden." Yankee.
　　　57.5 (May 1993): 84. <u>Article First</u>. OCLC. Bailey
　　　Howe Library, U. Vermont. 2 Jun. 2005 <http://
　　　firstsearch.oclc.org>.

Give the print publication information, name the database (underlined), name of vendor, name of library, date of access, and URL.

32. Professional site

<u>Yellow Wall-Paper Site</u>. U of Texas. 1995. 4 Mar. 1998
　　　<http://www.cwrl.utexas.edu/~daniel/amlit/
　　　wallpaper/wallpaper.html>.

33. Government or institutional site

"Zebra Mussels in Vermont." Home page. State of
Vermont Agency of Natural Resources. 3 May
1998 <http://www.anr.state.vt.us/dec/waterq/
smcap.htm>.

34. Article in a journal

Erkkila, Betsy. "The Emily Dickinson Wars." The
Emily Dickinson Journal 5.2 (1996) 14 pars.
2 Feb. 1998 <http://www.colorado.edu/EDIS/
Journal>.

35. Book

Twain, Mark. The Adventures of Tom Sawyer.
Internet Wiretap Online Library. Carnegie
Mellon U. 4 Mar. 1998 <http://www.cs.cmu.edu/
Web/People/rgs/sawyr-table.html>.

36. Poem

Poe, Edgar Allan. "The Raven." American Review,
1845. The Poetry Archives. 4 Mar. 1998 <http://
tqd.advanced.org/3247/cgibin/dispgi?poet=
poe.Edgar&poem>.

37. Article in a reference database

"Jupiter." Britannica Online. Vers. 97.1.1 Mar. 1997.
Encyclopaedia Britannica. 29 Mar. 1998
<http://www.eb.com:180>.

38. Posting to a discussion list

"New Virginia Woolf Discussion List." Online
posting. 22 Feb. 1996. The Virginia Woolf
Society, Ohio State U. 4 Mar. 1998 <gopher://
dept.english.upenn.edu:70//OrO-1858-?Lists/
20th/vwoolf>.

39. E-mail, listserv, or newsgroup (Usenet) message

Superman. <superman@200.uvm.edu>. "Writing
Committee Meeting." Distribution list.
University of Vermont. 24 Jan. 2001.

MLA MLA MLA MLA

Include the author's name or Internet alias (if known, alias first, period) followed by the subject line (in quotation marks) and the date of the posting. Identify the type of communication (*Personal e-mail, Distribution list, Office communication*) before the access date. The source's e-mail address is optional, following the name in angle brackets; secure permission before including an e-mail address.

40. File transfer protocol (FTP), telnet, or gopher site

King, Jr., Martin Luther. "I Have a Dream Speech."
28 Aug. 1963. 30 Jan. 1996 <telnet://
ukanaix.cc.ukans.edu>.

Substitute the abbreviation *ftp, telnet,* or *gopher* for *http* before the site address.

41. Synchronous communications (MUD, MOO, IRC)

StoneHenger. The Glass Dragon MOO. 6 Feb. 2004.
Personal interview. 6 Feb. 2004 <telnet://
surf.tstc.edu>.

Synchronous communications take place in real time; when they are over, an archive copy may remain, or they may simply be erased. After the posting date, include the type of discussion (e.g., *Personal interview, Group discussion*) followed by a period.

42. Home page—personal

Fulwiler, Anna. Home page. 1 Feb. 1998 <http://
www.uvm.edu/~afulwile>.

43. Home page—college course or academic department

Hughes, Jeffrey. Fundamentals of Field Science.
Course home page. Sep.-Dec. 2005. Botany
department. University of Vermont, 6 May 2005
<http://www.uvm.edu/~plantbio/grad/fn>.

List instructor or department name, course or department title, the words *course* or *department home page;* for course offering add inclusive dates, department name, school, date of access, and URL.

44. Online newspaper

Sandomir, Richard. "Yankees Talk Trades in
  Broadcast Booth." <u>New York Times on the Web</u>
  4 Dec. 2001. 5 Dec. 2001 <http://www.nytimes
  .com/pages/business/media/index.html>.

45. Online magazine

Epperson, Sharon. "A New Way to Shop for a
  College." <u>Time.com</u> 4 Dec. 2001. 5 Dec. 2001
  <http://www.time.com/time/education/article/
  0,8599,183955,00.html>.

46. Online encyclopedia

<u>Stanford Encyclopedia of Philosophy</u>. Ed. Edward N.
  Zalta. 1995. Stanford U. 5 Dec. 2001 <http://
  plato.stanford.edu/contents.html>.

47. Online work of art

Van Gogh, Vincent. <u>The Olive Trees</u>. 1889. Museum
  of Modern Art, New York. 5 Dec. 2001 <http://
  www.moma.org/docs/collection/paintsculpt/
  recent/c463.htm>.

48. Online interview

Plaxco, Jim. Interview. Planetary Studies Foundation.
  Oct. 1992. 5 Dec. 2001 <http://www.planets
  .org/>.

49. Online film or film clip

Columbus, Chris, dir. <u>Harry Potter and the Sorcerer's
  Stone</u>. Trailer. Warner Brothers, 2001. 5 Dec.
  2001 <http://hollywood.com>.

50. Online cartoon

Bell, Darrin. "Rudy Park." Cartoon. <u>New York Times
  on the Web</u> 5 Dec. 2001. 5 Dec. 2001 <http://
  www2.uclick.com/client/nyt/rk/>.

51. Electronic television or radio program

Chayes, Sarah. "Concorde." All Things Considered.
  Natl. Public Radio. 26 July 2000. 7 Dec. 2001
  <http://www.npr.com/programs/atc/archives>.

MLA MLA MLA MLA

52. Weblog entry

> Rickey, Anthony. "Three Years of Hell to Become the
>   Devil." Weblog posting. 8 June 2005. 10 June
>   2005 <http://www.threeyearsofhell.com/>.

Author name or pseudonym, title of site (if any) followed by the words "Weblog posting," date of site, date of access, and URL.

28 e   Documenting other sources

53. Cartoon, titled or untitled

> Roberts, Victoria. Cartoon. <u>New Yorker</u> 13 July
>   2000: 34.

54. Film or videocassette

> <u>Casablanca</u>. Dir. Michael Curtiz. Perf. Humphrey
>   Bogart and Ingrid Bergman. Warner Bros.,
>   1942.
> <u>Fast Food: What's in It for You</u>. Prod. Center for
>   Science. Videocassette. Los Angeles:
>   Churchill, 1988.

Begin with the title, followed by the director, the studio, and the year released. You may also include the names of lead actors, the producer, and the like between the title and the distribution information. If your essay is concerned with a particular person's work on a film, lead with that person's name, arranging all other information accordingly.

> Lewis, Joseph H., dir. <u>Gun Crazy</u>. Screenplay by
>   Dalton Trumbo. King Bros., 1950.

55. Personal interview

> Holden, James. Personal interview. 12 Jan. 2000.

Begin with the interviewee's name and specify the kind of interview and the date.

> Morser, John. Professor of Political Science, U of
>   Wisconsin. Telephone interview. 15 Dec. 2005.

56. Published or broadcast interview

> Steingass, David. Interview. <u>Counterpoint</u> 7 May
>   1970: 3-4.

For published or broadcast interviews, begin with the interviewee's name. Include appropriate publication information for a periodical or book and appropriate broadcast information for a radio or television program.

57. Print advertisement

> Cadillac DeVille. Advertisement. <u>New York Times</u>
> 21 Feb. 1996, natl. ed.: A20.

Begin with the name of the product, followed by the description *Advertisement* and publication information for the source.

58. Unpublished lecture, public address, or speech

> Graves, Donald. "When Bad Things Happen to Good
> Ideas." National Council of Teachers of
> English Convention. St. Louis. 21 Nov. 1989.

Begin with the speaker, followed by the title (if any), the meeting (and sponsoring organization, if needed), the location, and the date. If no title, use a descriptive label (*Speech*) with no quotation marks.

59. Personal or unpublished letter

> Friedman, Paul. Letter to the author. 18 Mar. 1998.

Begin with the name of the writer, identify the type of communication (for example, *E-mail* or *Letter*), and specify the audience. Include the date written, if known, or the date received.

To cite an unpublished letter from an archive or private collection, include information that locates the holding (for example, *Quinn-Adams Papers. Lexington Historical Society. Lexington, KY*).

60. Published letter

> King, Jr., Martin Luther. "Letter from Birmingham
> Jail." 28 Aug. 1963. <u>Civil Disobedience in
> Focus</u>. Ed. Hugo Adam Bedau. New York:
> Routledge, 1991. 68-84.

Specify the audience in the letter title (if known). Include the date immediately after the title. Place the page number(s) after the publisher information. If citing more than one letter from a collection, cite the entire collection in the

Works Cited list, and indicate individual dates and page numbers in your text.

61. Map

> <u>Ohio River: Foster, KY, to New Martinsville, WV</u>.
>   Map. Huntington: U.S. Army Corps of
>   Engineers, 1985.

Underline the title, and identify the source as a map or chart.

62. Performance

> Bissex, Rachel. Folk Songs. Flynn Theater.
>   Burlington, VT. 14 May 1990.

Identify title, place, and date of performance. If focusing on a particular person, such as the director or conductor, lead with that person's name. For a recital or individual concert, lead with the performer's name.

63. Audio recording

> Young, Neil, comp., perf. <u>Mirror Ball</u>. In part
>   accompanied by members of Pearl Jam.
>   Burbank: Reprise, 1995.

> Marley, Bob, and the Wailers. "Buffalo Soldier."
>   <u>Legend</u>. Audiocassette. Island Records, 1984.

Begin with the artist, composer, or conductor as appropriate. Enclose song titles in quotation marks, followed by the recording title, underlined. If not citing a compact disc, specify the recording format. End with the company label, the catalog number (if known), and the date of issue.

64. Television or radio broadcast

> "Emissary." <u>Star Trek: Deep Space Nine</u>. Teleplay
>   by Michael Pillar. Story by Rick Berman and
>   Michael Pillar. Dir. David Carson. Fox. WFLX,
>   West Palm Beach. 9 Jan. 1993.

If the broadcast is not an episode of a series or the episode is untitled, begin with the program title, underlined. Include the network, the station and city, and the date of the broadcast. The inclusion of other information such as narrator, writer, director, or performers depends on the purpose of your citation.

65. Work of art

Holbein, Hans. <u>Portrait of Erasmus</u>. The Louvre,
>   Paris. <u>The Louvre Museum</u>. By Germain Bazin.
>   New York: Abrams, n.d. 148.

Begin with the artist's name. Follow with the title, and conclude with the location. If your source is a book, include
pertinent publication information (slide, plate, figure information, page number).

29 | *Sample Works Cited Page in MLA Style*

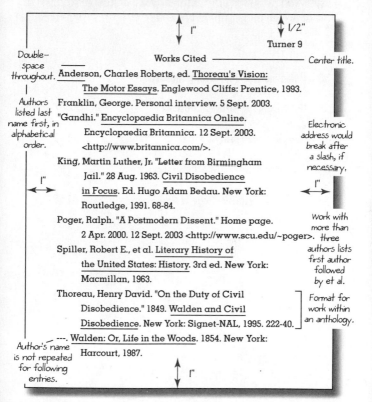

Sample Works Cited Page of a Student Essay in MLA Format

six

APA Documentation

Most disciplines in the social sciences and related fields use the name-and-date system of documentation put forth by the American Psychological Association (APA). The disciplines of education and business also use this system. This citation style highlights dates of publication because the currency of published material is of primary importance in these disciplines. Because collaborative authoring is common in the social sciences, listing the first six authors fully in the References is the current standard. For more about the foundations and purposes of the APA system, see the *Publication Manual of the American Psychological Association,* 5th ed. (Washington: APA, 2001) or the APA Web page http://www.apa.org/.

30 | *Guidelines for Formatting Manuscripts*

The APA *Publication Manual* integrates the widespread use of word processors for research, writing, and publication in its guidelines for professionals as well as students. The current standards permit the scholarly use of the special typeface and character options available on most word processors, thus bringing the college writing standards more in line with professional publications. This means that italic typeface rather than underlining is recommended for titles, emphasis, and so on. You will also note other standard publishing features in the models, such as the solid long (or em) dash instead of two hyphens. However, the *Manual* recommends caution: Overuse of font size or design options is never appropriate. Use good judgment, and always ask your instructor about any style or information display preferences he or she requires.

Paper and Printing

Print all academic assignments on clean, white 8½-by-11-inch paper in a standard serif font (e.g., Times New Roman, Courier) and point size (11–12) using a good-quality printer.

Margins and Spacing

Allow margins of one inch all around. Justify the left margin only. Double-space everything, including headings, quoted material, and the References page. Indent the first line of each paragraph five spaces or one-half inch.

For prose quotations of more than forty words, indent each line five spaces or one-half inch from the left margin. Do not use quotation marks to mark the beginning and end of such passages. Page numbers in parentheses are placed at the end of the passage, following ending punctuation. (*pp. 34–41*).

Page Numbers

Set page numbers to print in the upper right margin of all pages one-half inch below the top of the paper (including title page and abstract). APA format requires a shortened title (two to three words) five spaces before each page number to guarantee correct identification of stray pages (*Green Is 1, Green Is 2,* etc.).

Title Page

Page 1 of an APA-style paper is the title page. Center the title fifteen lines from the top; immediately below, type your name, the course name, your instructor's name, and the date, all centered. Use conventional title case punctuation (capitalizing key words only). Avoid using italics, underlining, quotation marks, boldface, unusual fonts, or an enlarged point size for the title.

Abstract

Page 2 is the abstract page. Center the word *Abstract* one inch from the top of the page; double-space to the abstract text and throughout. Write a 75- to 100-word (never exceed 120 words) paragraph that states your thesis and the main supporting points in clear, concise, descriptive language. Avoid statements of personal opinion and inflammatory judgments.

First Page of Text

On the page following the abstract, center the title of your paper at the top, double-space to the first line of text, and continue double-spacing throughout.

Punctuation

Use one space after periods, commas, semicolons, colons, question marks, exclamation points, and between the periods in an ellipsis. Long (em) dashes, with no extra spaces on either side, indicate interruptions within a sentence. Short (en) dashes abbreviate the word *to* in page ranges (*pp. 51–64*).

Visual Information

APA requires the labeling of all tables (charts) and figures (drawings, graphs, photographs, etc.) included in the text. Each is numbered in order as *Table 1* or *Figure 1,* and so on. Include a clear title and caption for each and place in the text as near as possible to the passage it refers to. In your text, be sure to discuss or identify the most important information or feature in each table or figure included.

31 | *Guidelines for In-Text Citations*

The following guidelines illustrate how to cite refer-ence material in the main body of your paper.

1. Single work by one or more authors

When quoting, paraphrasing, or summarizing material, give both the author's last name and the date of the source. For direct quotations, provide specific page numbers; for par-aphrases, page citations are optional. Page references in the APA system are preceded, in text or reference list (except for journal articles), by the abbreviation *p.* or *pp.*

Supply authors' names, publication dates, and page numbers (when listed) in parentheses following the cited material. Do not repeat any of these elements if you iden-tify them in the text preceding the parenthetical citation.

> Exotoxins make some bacteria dangerous to humans (Thomas, 1974).

> According to Thomas (1974), "Some bacteria are harmful to us only if they make exotoxins" (p. 76).

> We need fear some bacteria only "if they make exotoxins" (Thomas, 1974, p. 76).

For a work by two authors, cite both names.

> Smith and Rogers (1990) agree that all bacteria producing exotoxins are harmful to humans.

> All known exotoxin-producing bacteria are harmful to humans (Smith & Rogers, 1990).

The authors' names are joined by *and* in the text, but use an ampersand (&) to join authors' names within parenthe-ses and on the References page.

For a work by three to five authors, identify all the au-thors by last name the first time the citation occurs. In sub-sequent references, identify only the first author followed by *et al.* ("and others").

> The most recent study supports the belief that alcohol abuse is on the rise (Dinkins, Dominic, & Smith, 1989).

When homeless people were excluded from the study, the results were the same (Dinkins et al., 1989).

If citing a source by six or more authors, identify only the first author in all the in-text references, followed by *et al.* (See Chapter 33 for References page guidelines.)

2. Two or more works by the same author(s) published in the same year

To distinguish between two or more works published in the same year by the same author(s), organize the entries alphabetically by title; then assign a lowercase letter (*a, b, c,* etc.) to each, in sequence, immediately after the date. (These letters will appear after the date in the References as well.) If two such works appear in one citation, repeat the year.

> (Smith, 1992a, 1992b)

3. Unknown author

To cite the work of an unknown author, identify the first two or three words of the entry as listed on the References page. If the words are from the title, enclose them in quotation marks or italicize them, as appropriate.

> The literacy rate for Mexico was 75% in 1990, up 4% from a decade earlier (*Statistical Abstracts,* 1991).

4. Corporate or organizational author

Spell out the name of the authoring agency for a work by a corporation, association, organization, or foundation. If the name can be abbreviated and remain identifiable, you may spell out the full name the first time, with the abbreviation or acronym in brackets immediately after it. For subsequent references, use only the abbreviation.

> (American Psychological Association [APA], 2007)
>
> (APA, 2007)

5. Authors with the same last name

To avoid confusion in citing two or more authors with the same last name, include each author's initials in every citation.

(J. M. Clark, 2005)

(C. L. Clark, 2006)

6. Quotation from an indirect source

Use the words *as cited in* for quotations or information from your source but originally from another source.

> Lester Brown of Worldwatch believes that
> international agriculture production has reached
> its limit and that "we're going to be in trouble on
> the food front before this decade is out" (as cited
> in Mann, 1993, p. 51).

7. More than one work in a citation

List two or more sources within a single parenthetical citation in the same order in which they appear in your References list. If you refer to two or more works by the same author, list them in chronological order, with the author's name mentioned once and the dates separated by commas.

> (Thomas, 1974, 1979)

List works by different authors in alphabetical order by the author's last name, separated by semicolons.

> (Miller, 1990; Webster & Rose, 1988)

8. A Web site

When citing an entire Web site but not a specific document, page, text, or figure from the site, include the Web address in the text or in parentheses.

> To locate information about the University of
> Vermont faculty, visit the school's Web site
> (http://www.uvm.edu).

When the name and Web address are included in the text, no References entry is needed.

9. Specific information from a Web site

Cite specific information (author, figure, table, paraphrased or quoted passage) from a Web site by including the brief author–date information in the text or in parentheses, followed by complete information on the References page.

10. Setting off a long quotation from text

Start quotations of forty or more words on a new line, and indent the entire block one-half inch from the left-hand margin. Indent the first line of the second or any subsequent paragraphs (but not the first paragraph) five additional spaces. Double-space all such quotations, omit quotation marks, and place the parenthetical citation after end punctuation, with no period following the citation.

11. Footnotes

Numbered footnotes provide additional information of interest to some readers but are also likely to slow the pace of your text or obscure your point for other readers.

Make footnotes as brief as possible; when the information you wish to add is extensive, present it in an appendix.

Number footnotes consecutively (as they have been in your text), and present them on a page headed by the word *Notes* before the References list. Type all footnotes double-spaced, and indent the first line of each as you would a paragraph.

32   *Sample Pages in APA Style*

The research essay "Green Is Only Skin Deep: False Environmental Marketing" by Elizabeth Bone was written in response to an assignment to identify and explain one problem in contemporary American culture. Bone's essay is documented according to the conventions of the American Psychological Association (APA). This excerpt includes the title page, abstract, and first page. Ask your instructor if a separate title page and/or an abstract are required for your course.

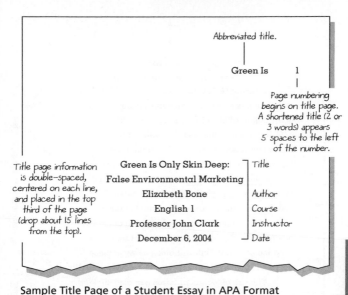

Abbreviated title.

Green Is   1

Page numbering begins on title page. A shortened title (2 or 3 words) appears 5 spaces to the left of the number.

Title page information is double-spaced, centered on each line, and placed in the top third of the page (drop about 15 lines from the top).

Green Is Only Skin Deep: Title
False Environmental Marketing
Elizabeth Bone   Author
English 1   Course
Professor John Clark   Instructor
December 6, 2004   Date

Sample Title Page of a Student Essay in APA Format

Abstract is placed on a separate page following the title page.

1"   1/2"

Green Is   2

Abstract ——— Heading is centered.

Double-space throughout.

No paragraph indent. Most Americans consider themselves environmentalists and favor supporting environmentally friendly or "green" companies. However, companies use a number of false advertising practices to mislead the public about their green practices and products by (1) exaggerating claims, (2) masking false practices behind technical terminology, (3) mis-sponsoring green events, (4) not admitting responsibility for real problems, (5) advertising green by association, and (6) solving one problem while creating others. Consumers must be skeptical of all commercial ads and take the time to find out the truth behind advertising.

Abstract summarizes the main points of the paper.

Abstract points follow the order in the paper.

Sample Abstract Page of a Student Essay in APA Format

Title is repeated from title page and is centered. Double-space throughout.

Author last names and date are included in text.

APA APA APA

1"

Green Is   3

Abbreviated title followed by page number on all pages.

Green Is Only Skin Deep:
False Environmental Marketing

A recent Gallup poll reported that "75% of Americans consider themselves to be environmentalists" (Smith & Quelch, 1993, p. 9). In the same study, nearly half of the respondents said they would be more likely to purchase a product if they perceived it to be environmentally friendly, or "green." According to Smith and Quelch (1993), because green sells, many companies have begun to promote themselves as marketing products that are either environmentally friendly or manufactured from recycled material. Unfortunately, many of these companies care more about appearance than reality.

Informational thesis at end of first paragraph.

The use of technical terms can also mislead average consumers. For example, carbon fluoride compounds, called CFCs, are known to be hazardous to the protective layer of ozone that surrounds the earth, so their widespread use in air conditioners is considered an environmental hazard (Decker & Stammer, 1989). Chrysler Corporation advertises that it uses CFC-free refrigerant in its automobile air conditioners to appeal to environmentally concerned consumers ("Ozone Layer," 1994). However, Weisskopf (1992) points out that "the chemical compounds that replace CFCs in their air conditioners pose other environmental hazards that are not mentioned" (pp. 91–92).

Example of misleading advertising introduced.

Sample First Page of a Student Essay in APA Format

33 | Guidelines for the APA References Page

All works mentioned in a paper should be identified on a reference list according to the following general rules of the APA documentation system.

33 a   Format

After the final page of the paper, title a separate page *References* with no italics, underlining, or quotation marks. Center the title one inch from the top of the page. Number the page in sequence with the last page of the paper.

Double-space throughout—between the title and the first entry as well as between and within entries. Set the first line flush with the left-hand margin.

Indent the second and all subsequent lines of an entry five spaces (or one default tab) from the left margin in a hanging indent. The paragraph indent format, with the first line indented five spaces, is no longer acceptable.

Do not repeat the title *References* when your reference list exceeds one page.

Alphabetize the list of references according to authors' last names, using the first author's last name for works with multiple authors. For entries by an unknown author, alphabetize by the first word of the title, ignoring an initial *A, An,* or *The.*

33 b   Documenting books

Following are examples of the reference list format for a variety of source types using standard APA hanging indent format.

1. Book by one author

> Benjamin, J. (1988). *The bonds of love: Psychoanalysis, feminism, and the problem of domination.* New York: Prometheus.

Use italics, not underlining, to indicate titles of books.

2. Book by two or more authors

> Zweigenhaft, R. L., & Domhoff, G. W. (1991). *Blacks in the white establishment?: A study of race and class in America.* New Haven, CT: Yale University Press.

Include all authors' names in the reference list, regardless of the number of authors associated with a particular work.

3. More than one book by the same author

List two or more works by the same author(s) chronologically by year, earliest work first. Arrange any such works published in the same year alphabetically by title, placing lowercase letters after the dates. In either case, give full identification of author(s) for each reference listing.

> Bandura, A. (1969). *Principles of behavior modification*. New York: Holt, Rinehart, and Winston.

> Bandura, A. (1977a). Self-efficacy: Toward a unifying theory of behavioral change. *Psychological Review, 84,* 191–215.

> Bandura, A. (1977b). *Social learning theory.* Englewood Cliffs, NJ: Prentice Hall.

If the same author is named first but listed with different coauthors, alphabetize by the last name of the second author. Works by the first author alone are listed before works with coauthors.

4. Book by a corporation, association, organization, or foundation

> American Psychological Association. (2001). *Publication manual of the American Psychological Association* (5th ed.). Washington: Author.

Alphabetize corporate authors by the corporate name, excluding the articles *A, An,* and *The.* When the corporate author is also the publisher, designate the publisher as *Author.*

5. Revised edition of a book

> Peek, S. (1993). *The game inventor's handbook* (Rev. ed.). Cincinnati, OH: Betterway.

6. Edited book

> Schaefer, C. E., & Reid, S. E. (Eds.). (1986). *Game play: Therapeutic use of childhood games.* New York: Wiley.

Place *Ed.* or *Eds.,* capitalized, after the editor(s) of an edited book.

7. Book in more than one volume

> Waldrep, T. (Ed.). (1985–1988). *Writers on writing*
> (Vols. 1–2). New York: Random House.

For a work with volumes published in different years, indicate the range of dates of publication. If you referred to only one volume of a multivolume work, indicate only the volume cited.

> Waldrep, T. (Ed.). (1988). *Writers on writing* (Vol. 2).
> New York: Random House.

8. Translated or reprinted book

> Freud, S. (1950). *The interpretation of dreams* (A. A.
> Brill, Trans.). New York: Modern Library-
> Random House. (Original work published
> 1900)

Cite date of the translation or reprint in parentheses after the author's name. Place the original publication date in parentheses at the end of the citation, with no period. In the parenthetical citation in your text, include both dates: (*Freud 1900/1950*).

9. Chapter or article in an edited book

> Telander, R. (1996). Senseless crimes. In C. I.
> Schuster & W. V. Van Pelt (Eds.), *Speculations:*
> *Readings in culture, identity, and values* (2nd
> ed., pp. 264–272). Upper Saddle River, NJ:
> Prentice Hall.

The chapter or article title is not underlined or in quotation marks. Editors' names are listed in normal reading order (surname last). Inclusive page numbers, in parentheses, follow the book title.

10. Anonymous book

> *Stereotypes, distortions and omissions in U.S. history*
> *textbooks.* (1977). New York: Council on
> Interracial Books for Children.

11. Government document

> U.S. House of Representatives, Committee on
> Energy and Commerce. (1986). *Ensuring access*

to programming for the backyard satellite
dish owner (Serial No. 99-127). Washington:
U.S. Government Printing Office.

Provide the higher department or governing agency only when the office or agency that created the document is not readily recognizable. If a document number is available, list it in parentheses after the document title. Write out the name of the printing agency in full rather than using the abbreviation *GPO*.

33 c Documenting periodicals

In citing periodical articles, use the same format for listing author names as for books.

12. Article in a journal paginated by volume

Hartley, J. (1991). Psychology, writing, and
computers: A review of research. *Visible
Language, 25*, 339–375.

If page numbers are continuous throughout volumes in a year, use only the volume number, italicized, following the title of the periodical. Do not use the abbreviation *p.* or *pp.* unless there is no volume number.

13. Article in a journal paginated by issue

Lowther, M. A. (1977). Career change in mid-life: Its
impact on education. *Innovator, 8*(7), 1, 9–11.

Include the issue number in parentheses if each issue of a journal is paginated separately. Do not use the abbreviation *p.* or *pp.* unless there is no volume number.

14. Magazine article

Garreau, J. (1995, December). Edgier cities. *Wired*,
pp. 158–163, 232–234.

For nonprofessional periodicals, include the year and month (not abbreviated) after the author's name. Use the abbreviation *p.* or *pp.* unless there is a volume number.

15. Newspaper article

> Finn, P. (1995, September 27). Death of a U-Va.
> student raises scrutiny of off-campus
> drinking. *The Washington Post,* pp. D1, D4.

If an author is listed, begin with the author's name, then list the date (spell out the month); follow article title with the newspaper title. Combine section number or letter with the page number(s), using the abbreviation *p.* or *pp.* If the name of the newspaper includes the word *the,* capitalize and italicize it also.

APA conventions for documenting sources such as CD-ROMs, diskettes, and magnetic tapes list author, date, and title followed by the complete information for the corresponding print source, if available.

16. CD-ROM

> Krauthammer, C. (1991). Why is America in a blue
> funk? *Time, 138,* 83. Retrieved from UMIACH
> database (Periodical Abstracts, CD-ROM Item:
> 1126.00).

17. Computer software

> HyperCard (Version 2.2) [Computer software]. (1993).
> Cupertino, CA: Apple Computer.

Provide the version number, if available, in parentheses following the program or software name. Add the descriptive term *Computer software* in brackets, and follow it with a period. Do not italicize the names of computer programs.

33 d Documenting online sources

Online Sources

An APA Internet citation should provide essentially the same information as any textual source: author (when identified), date of site creation, title (or description of document), date of retrieval, and a working address (URL).

Try to reference specific documents or links, whenever possible, rather than general home or menu pages, because such pages commonly contain many links, only one of which you are citing.

To transcribe a URL correctly, keep your word processing file open and copy the URL directly from the Internet site to your paper. (Make sure your word processor's
automatic hyphenation feature is turned off because an
automatically inserted hyphen will change the URL; if you
need to break a URL, do so after a slash or before a period.) APA does not recommend using angle brackets to indicate an Internet address.

If electronic sources don't provide page numbers, use
paragraph numbers only if numbered in the document:
(*para 4*). If the source is divided into chapters, use chapter
and paragraph numbers: (*chap 2. 12*). If the source is divided into sections, use section and paragraph numbers to
identify the source location: *(section 6, 8)*.

For more details than the following examples can provide, consult the APA's Web page at http://www.apa.org/
journals/webref.html.

18. Online periodical article

Kapadia, S. (1995, November). A tribute to Mahatma
Gandhi: His views on women and social
exchange. *Journal of South Asia Women's
Studies, 1*(1). Retrieved December 2, 1995, from
http://www.shore.net/~india/jsaws

Indicate the number of paragraphs in brackets after the
title, and add the term [*On-line serial*] in brackets between
the journal name and the volume number. If you have
viewed the article only in its electronic form, add *Electronic
version* in brackets after the article title:

Smithsonian Institution's Ocean Planet: A special
report [Electronic version]. (1995). *Outdoor Life,
3*, 13–22. Retrieved November 1, 1999, from
http://www.epinions.com/mags-Outdoor Life

19. World Wide Web site

To document a specific file, list the author, the date of publication, and the titles of the document and the complete
work (if any). Add relevant information such as volume or
page numbers of a print source. Conclude with a retrieval
statement.

Williams, S. (1996, June 14). Back to school with the
quilt. *AIDS Memorial Quilt Website*. Retrieved

June 14, 1996, from http://www.aidsquilt.org/
newsletter/stories/backto.html

Start with the title if no author is identified.

> *GVU's 8th WWW user survey.* (n.d.). Retrieved August
> 8, 2000, from http://www.cc.gatech.edu/gvu/
> usersurveys/survey1997-10/

20. Work from an online database.

> Conniff, R. (May 1993). Approaching *Walden.*
> *Yankee, 57*(5), 84. Retrieved June 2, 2005, from
> ArticleFirst database.

Give the print publication information and when it was retrieved from which database. No URL is required.

21. Weblog entry

> Rickey, A. (8 June 2005). *Three years of hell to
> become the devil.* Retrieved June 10, 2005,
> from http://www.threeyearsofhell.com/

22. File transfer protocol (FTP), telnet, or gopher site

After the retrieval date, supply the FTP, telnet, or gopher
search path.

> Altar, T. W. (1993). *Vitamin B12 and vegans.* Retrieved
> May 28, 1996, from ftp://ftp.cs.yale.edu

> Clinton, W. (1994, July 17). Remarks by the President
> at the tribute dinner for Senator Byrd.
> Washington, DC: Office of the White House
> Press Secretary. Retrieved February 12, 1996,
> from gopher://info.tamu.edu.70/00/.data/
> politics/1994/byrd.0717

23. Synchronous communications (MOO, MUD, IRC)

To document a *real-time communication,* such as those
posted in MOOs, MUDs, and IRCs, describe the type of communication (e.g., *Group discussion, Personal interview*) if
it is not indicated elsewhere in the entry.

Harnack, A. (1996, April 4). Words [Group
discussion]. Retrieved April 5, 1996, from
telnet://moo.du.org/port=8888

24. Web discussion forum

Holden, J. B. (2001, January 2). The failure of higher
education [Formal discussion initiation].
Message posted to http://ifets.mtu.edu/
archives

25. Listserv (electronic mailing list)

Weston, H. (2002, June 12). Re: Registration schedule
now available. Message posted to the
Chamberlain Kronsage dormitory electronic
mailing list, archived at http://listserv
.registrar.uwsp.edu/archives/62.html

Note that APA prefers the term *electronic mailing list* to
listserv.

26. Newsgroup

Hotgirl. (2002, January 12). Dowsing effort fails.
Message posted to news://alt.science
.esp3/html

27. Electronic newspaper article

Kolata, G. (2002, February 12). Why some people
won't be fit despite exercise. *New York Times.*
Retrieved February 12, 2002, from http://www
.nytimes.com

28. Document available on university program or department Web site

McClintock, R., & Taipale, K. A. (1994). *Educating
America for the 21st century: A strategic
plan for educational leadership 1993–2001.*
Retrieved February 12, 2002, from Columbia

University, Institute for Learning Technologies
Web site: http://www.ilt.columbia.edu/ilt/
docs/ILTplan.html

29. E-mail messages

Under current APA guidelines, electronic conversations are
not listed on the References page. Cite e-mail messages in
the text as you would personal letters or interviews.

> R. W. Williams, personal communication, January 4,
> 2006.

Following is an in-text parenthetical reference to a personal e-mail message:

> R.W. Williams (personal communication, January 4,
> 2006) told me that the practice of dowsing has
> a scientific basis.

33 e   Documenting other sources

30. Motion picture, recording, and other nonprint media

> Curtiz, M. (Director). (1942). *Casablanca* [Motion
> picture]. United States: Warner Bros.

Alphabetize a motion picture listing by the name of the
person or persons with primary responsibility for the product. Identifying information about this person or persons,
such as the director, should appear in parentheses. Identify the medium in brackets following the title, and indicate
both location (country of origin for motion picture) and
name of the studio or distributor (as publisher).

31. Interviews and other field sources

These are identified in the text in parentheses (name, place,
date) but are not listed on the References page.

34

Sample References Page in APA Style

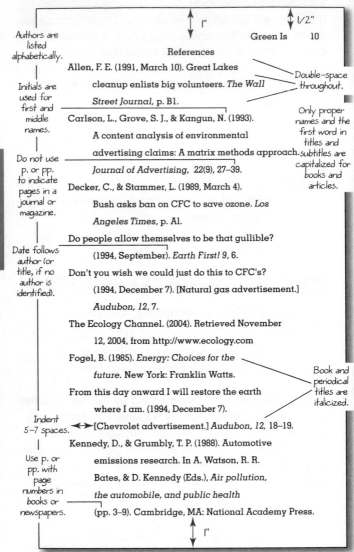

Authors are listed alphabetically.

Initials are used for first and middle names.

Do not use p. or pp. to indicate pages in a journal or magazine.

Date follows author (or title, if no author is identified).

Indent 5–7 spaces.

Use p. or pp. with page numbers in books or newspapers.

Double-space throughout.

Only proper names and the first word in titles and subtitles are capitalized for books and articles.

Book and periodical titles are italicized.

Green Is   10

References

Allen, F. E. (1991, March 10). Great Lakes
    cleanup enlists big volunteers. *The Wall
    Street Journal*, p. B1.

Carlson, L., Grove, S. J., & Kangun, N. (1993).
    A content analysis of environmental
    advertising claims: A matrix methods approach.
    Journal of Advertising, 22(9), 27–39.

Decker, C., & Stammer, L. (1989, March 4).
    Bush asks ban on CFC to save ozone. *Los
    Angeles Times*, p. A1.

Do people allow themselves to be that gullible?
    (1994, September). *Earth First! 9*, 6.

Don't you wish we could just do this to CFC's?
    (1994, December 7). [Natural gas advertisement.]
    Audubon, 12, 7.

The Ecology Channel. (2004). Retrieved November
    12, 2004, from http://www.ecology.com

Fogel, B. (1985). *Energy: Choices for the
    future*. New York: Franklin Watts.

From this day onward I will restore the earth
    where I am. (1994, December 7).
    [Chevrolet advertisement.] *Audubon, 12*, 18–19.

Kennedy, D., & Grumbly, T. P. (1988). Automotive
    emissions research. In A. Watson, R. R.
    Bates, & D. Kennedy (Eds.), *Air pollution,
    the automobile, and public health*
    (pp. 3–9). Cambridge, MA: National Academy Press.

Sample References Page of a Student Essay in APA Format

The most widely used documentation system in history, philosophy, religion, and the fine arts is that of the *Chicago Manual of Style,* 15th edition (Chicago: University of Chicago Press, 2003). The *Chicago Manual* (CM) style places numbers in the text that correspond to notes at either the bottom of the page (footnotes) or the end of the paper (endnotes). Because citations are signaled only by small raised numbers, CM style calls less attention to documentation than the parenthetical in-text systems of MLA and APA.

35   *Guidelines for Formatting Manuscripts*

T he CM guidelines for preparing manuscripts do not reflect the wealth of visually interesting options in fonts, point sizes, visual insertions, and other features available on modern word processing programs. If your instructor requests strict CM format, follow the guidelines here. If your instructor encourages more creative formats, use good judgment in displaying the information in your text. The following guidelines describe the preparation of the main body of your paper.

Paper and Printing

Print all academic assignments on clean, white 8½-by-11-inch paper in a standard font (e.g., Times New Roman, Courier) and point size (11–12) using a good-quality printer.

Margins and Spacing

Allow margins of one inch all around. Justify the left margin only. Use the tab key to indent the first line of each paragraph.

For prose quotations of more than one paragraph (or two lines of poetry), use the indent key to indent the entire quotation. Do not use quotation marks with such passages.

Double-space everything in the paper, including headings, quoted material, notes, and Bibliography entries.

Page Numbers

Set page numbers to print in the upper right margin of all pages, one-half inch below the top of the paper; do not use the word *page* or the abbreviation *p.* with page numbers. It is optional to include your last name before each page number—a protection in case pages become separated from the manuscript. Count but do not number the title page, so the first page of text begins with number 2.

Title Page

Attach an unnumbered title page. Center the title fifteen lines from the top. Four spaces below the title, center the word *By;* two spaces below that, center your name, the course name, your instructor's name, and the date.

First Page of Text

Center the title on the first page using conventional title case punctuation (capitalizing key words only). If your instructor asks for strict CM style, avoid using italics, underlining, quotation marks, boldface, unusual fonts, or an enlarged point size for the title. Double-space to the first paragraph and continue double-spacing throughout.

Punctuation

Use one space after commas, semicolons, colons, periods, question marks, exclamation points, and between the periods in an ellipsis.

Visual Information

Number all tables (charts, graphs) and figures (drawings, photographs) sequentially. Write a clear caption for each. Submit each on a separate unnumbered page inserted in your manuscript immediately following the point in the text it illustrates. At that point in the text, insert a reference to the table ("see table 1") or figure ("see fig. 2").

36 | *Guidelines for In-Text Citations*

36 a   Acknowledging sources

In the main body of the paper, mark each quotation, paraphrase, and summary of source material by inserting a raised (superscript) Arabic number immediately after the sentence or clause. The superscript number follows all punctuation except dashes. Numbers run consecutively throughout the text.

> Frank Lloyd Wright's "prairie style" was characterized by the houses he built in and around Chicago "with low horizontal lines echoing the landscape."[1] Vincent Scully sees these suburban buildings as one of Wright's most important influences.[2]

For each superscript number, write a corresponding note, either at the end of the paper (an endnote, on a separate page titled Notes) or at the foot of the page on which the number appears (a footnote).

1. *The Concise Columbia Encyclopedia*, 3rd ed., s.v. "Wright, Frank Lloyd."

2. Vincent Scully, *Architecture: The Natural and the Manmade* (New York: St. Martin's Press, 1991), 340.

36 b Bibliography

A Bibliography is required at the end of a Chicago-style paper. It lists all of the works you consulted in writing the paper, whether or not actually cited in a footnote or endnote. When you use endnotes, the Bibliography follows. Following are guidelines for assembling the Bibliography.

- Center the word *Bibliography* at the top of the page.
- Type the first line of each entry flush with the left margin.
- List all authors or editors in alphabetical order, last names first.
- List the names of coauthors in normal order, first names first, separated by commas.
- If two or more authors share the same last name, alphabetize by first name.
- If two or more works are by the same author, alphabetize by the title of the work. After the first listing, use a three-em dash to indicate the author's name for each subsequent work.
- If neither author nor editor is listed, alphabetize by title.
- Use periods followed by one space to separate the author from the title from the publication data.
- Capitalize all important words in the title.
- Underline or italicize the titles of published books, periodicals, or films.
- Use quotation marks to indicate the titles of articles, chapters, poems, and stories within published books.
- The entries in the Bibliography appear the same as they do on the Notes page, except that they are in

alphabetical, not numerical, order and the name of the first (or sole) author is inverted (see Chapter 37).

---

37 | *Guidelines for Endnote/ Footnote Citation*

E ndnotes are typed as one double-spaced list at the end of the text. The endnote format is easy to deal with, and it allows you to add or delete notes and change numbering with less fuss than footnotes entail.

The endnotes follow the last page of text, starting on a new page numbered in sequence. The title Notes is centered without quotation marks, one inch from the top of the page. Double-space before the first entry, within entries, and between entries. List entries in the order of the note numbers in your paper. Indent the first line of each note.

Footnotes enable readers to find information at a glance. Footnotes are placed at the bottom of the page on which the superscript numbers referring to them appear, four lines of space below the last line of text on that page.

Numbers in footnotes are aligned with the entry, followed by a period and one space before the first word. Indent each note.

A Bibliography is normally required to provide readers with a convenient way of identifying an author's full set of sources (see 36b).

CM CM CM

---

37 a   Documenting books: First reference

1. Book by one author

1. Lewis Thomas, *Lives of a Cell: Notes of a Biology Watcher* (New York: Viking, 1974), 76.

2. Book by two or more authors

2. Toby Fulwiler and Alan R. Hayakawa, *The Blair Handbook*, 3rd ed. (Upper Saddle River, NJ: Prentice Hall, 2000), 234.

3. Revised edition of a book

3. S. I. Hayakawa, *Language in Thought and Action,* 4th ed. (New York: Harcourt, 1978), 77.

4. Edited book and one volume of a multivolume book

4. Tom Waldrep, ed., *Writers on Writing,* vol. 2 (New York: Random House, 1988), 123.

5. Translated book

5. Albert Camus, *The Stranger,* trans. Stuart Gilbert (New York: Random House, 1946), 12.

6. Reprinted book

6. Zora Neale Hurston, *Their Eyes Were Watching God* (1937; reprint, New York: Perennial-Harper, 1990), 32.

7. Work in an anthology or edited collection

7. John Donne, "The Good-Morrow," in *The Metaphysical Poets,* ed. Helen Gardner (Baltimore: Penguin, 1957), 58.

8. Article in a reference book

8. *The Concise Columbia Encyclopedia,* 1998 ed., s.v. "Behn, Aphra."

An alphabetically arranged book requires no page numbers.

9. Anonymous book

9. *The World Almanac and Book of Facts* (New York: World Almanac-Funk & Wagnalls, 1995).

37 b Documenting periodicals

10. Article, story, or poem in a monthly or bimonthly magazine

10. Robert A. Linn and Stephen B. Dunbar, "The Nation's Report Card Goes Home," *Phi Delta Kappan,* October 2000, 127–43.

11. Article, story, or poem in a weekly magazine

11. Alex Ross, "The Wanderer," *New Yorker*, 10 May 1999, 56–63.

12. Article in a daily newspaper

12. Jane E. Brody, "Doctors Get Poor Marks for Nutrition Knowledge," *New York Times*, 10 February 1992, p. B7.

13. "Redistricting Reconsidered," *Washington Post*, 12 May 1992, p. B2.

13. Article in a journal paginated by volume

14. Joseph Harris, "The Other Reader," *Journal of Advanced Composition* 12 (1992): 34–36.

14. Article in a journal paginated by issue

15. Helen Tiffin, "Post-Colonialism, Post-Modernism, and the Rehabilitation of Post-Colonial History," *Journal of Commonwealth Literature* 23, no. 1 (1988): 189–95.

15. Review

16. Mimi Kramer, "Victims." Review of *'Tis Pity She's a Whore*, as performed at the New York Shakespeare Festival, *New Yorker*, 20 April 1992, 78–79.

37 c Documenting online sources

To document a site on the World Wide Web, provide the following information.

- Author's name
- Title of document in quotation marks
- Title of complete work (if relevant) in italics or underlined
- Date of publication or latest revision (day/month/year) if available

- Date of access in parentheses (accessed day/ month/year)
- Include end punctuation following a URL as needed.

16. Published Web site

17. Jonathon L. Beller, "What's Inside *The Insider?*" *Pop Matters Film,* 1999, http://popmatters .com/film/insider.html (accessed 21 May 2000).

17. Personal Web site

18. Toby Fulwiler, "Homepage," 2 Apr. 2000, http://www.uvm.edu/~tfulwile (accessed 6 May 2000).

18. Professional Web site

19. *Yellow Wall-Paper Site,* University of Texas, 1995, http://www.cwrl.utexas.edu/~daniel/amlit/ wallpaper/ (accessed 12 August 2006).

19. Publication reprinted on the Web

20. Betsy Erkkila, "The Emily Dickinson Wars," *The Emily Dickinson Journal* 5.2 (1996), 14 pars., 8 November 1998, http://www.colorado.edu/EDIS/ Journal (accessed 2 June 1999).

20. Article in a reference database

21. "Victorian," *Britannica Online,* Vers. 97.1, 1 March 1997, *Encyclopaedia Britannica,* http:// www.eb.com:180 (accessed 3 May 2004).

21. E-mail or listserv message

22. Toby Fulwiler, "A Question About Electronic Sources," E-mail to author, University of Vermont (23 May 2005).

37 d   Documenting other sources

22. Personal interview

23. John Morser, interview by author,
15 December 1999.

23. Personal or unpublished letter

24. Paul Friedman, letter to author, 18 March 1998.

24. Work of art

25. Hans Holbein, *Portrait of Erasmus,* The
Louvre, Paris, page 148 in *The Louvre Museum,*
by Germain Bazin (New York: Abrams, n.d.).

37 e   Documenting subsequent references

25. Subsequent references to a work

The second and any subsequent times you refer to a source,
include the author's last name followed by a comma,
a shortened version of the title, a comma, and the page
number(s).

26. Thomas, *Lives,* 99.

38 | *Sample Endnote/Footnote Pages in CM Style*

↕ I"

Owsley 2

recorded "in exultant tones the universal
neglect that had overtaken pagan learning."[2] It
would be some time, however, before Christian
education would replace classical training, and
by the fourth century, a lack of interest in
learning and culture among the elite of Roman
society was apparent. Attempting to check
the demise of education, the later emperors
established municipal schools, and universities
of rhetoric and law were also established in major
cities throughout the Empire.[3]

Superscript numbers indicate source references.

↕ I"

Owsley 12

Notes

Individual note entries are double-spaced throughout.

1. Rosamond McKitterick, *The Carolingians and the Written Word* (Cambridge: Cambridge University Press, 1983), 61.

First line indents.

2. J. Bass Mullinger, *The Schools of Charles the Great* (New York: Stechert, 1911), 10.

3. James W. Thompson, *The Literacy of the Laity in the Middle Ages* (New York: Franklin, 1963), 17.

4. 0. M. Dalton, introduction, *The Letters of Sidonius* (Oxford: Clarendon, 1915), cxiv.

5. Pierre Riche, *Education and Culture in the Barbarian West* (Columbia: University of South Carolina Press, 1976), 4.

6. Thompson, *Literacy of the Laity*, 17.

Separate page(s) at end of paper include all references in numerical order.

Subsequent reference to a work requires only author last name or names, shortened title, and page number.

Sample Pages of a Student Essay with Endnotes in CM Style

Kelly 5

1"

The Teatro Olimpico was completed in 1564, the statues, inscriptions, and bas-reliefs for the *fronsscena* being the last details completed. Meanwhile, careful plans were made for an inaugural, which was to be a production of *Oedipus* in a new translation.[10] Final decisions were made by the Academy in February 1585 for the seating of city officials, their wives, and others, with the ruling that "no masked men or women would be allowed in the theatre for the performance." [11] The organization of the audience space was "unique among Renaissance theaters, suggesting . . . its function as the theater of a 'club of equals,' rather than of a princely court."[12] The Academy is celebrated and related to Roman grandeur by the decoration over the monumental central opening, where its motto, 'Hoc Opus," appears.[13] It is difficult to make out the entrances.

Superscript numbers indicate reference.

Notes are numbered consecutively throughout the paper.

Number is repeated from the text and indented.

10. J. Thomas Oosting, *Andrea Palladio's Teatro Olimpico* (Ann Arbor: University of Michigan Research Press, 1981), 118.

If a source is the same as the immediately preceding work, use Ibid. and the page number.

11. Ibid., 120.

12. Marvin Carlson, *Places of Performance; The Semiotics of Theater Architecture* (Ithaca, Cornell University Press, 1989), 5.

13. Simon Tidworth, *Theaters: An Architectural and Cultural History* (London: Praeger, 1973), 52.

Double-space throughout.

CM CM CM

CM CM

Sample Page of a Student Essay with Footnotes in CM Style

PART

eight
Design and Presentation

The form in which you present your work depends, like your writing, on your purpose, your situation, and your audience. This section introduces some ideas about arranging words and images on paper, organizing information on the Internet, creating résumés, and preparing oral presentations. The objective in each case is to arrange your writing in a way that communicates clearly.

39 | *Designing Printed Documents*

Design is the process of arranging your writing for others to read. In a college paper, your objective is to present your work in a neat, attractive form that makes its organization apparent.

39 a Objectives of design

Good design is *transparent:* it calls attention to your work, not to itself. If a magazine cover catches your eye and you think, "I want to read that," the design is doing its job.

Here are some design objectives and ways to achieve them.

1. **Attract attention.** Choose layout, type font, illustrations, and graphics to spark interest.

2. **Create flow.** Make your document easy to read. Move background information or statistics to tables or boxes where they don't disrupt your narrative or argument.

3. **Show hierarchy.** Make similar items resemble one another (this list is an example). Consider subheadings or initial capitals to identify major sections.

4. **Reinforce contrast.** If your paper advances one side of an argument, consider summarizing the opposing view in a box or "sidebar."

5. **Use graphics.** Charts make numbers easier to understand. Drawings or photos can convey information more efficiently than words.

6. **Create emphasis.** A pull-out quotation calls attention to an important concept. Boldface type highlights key terms.

7. **Offer choices.** By displaying information outside the main text, you allow readers to choose whether to read background information, for example, or stay with your main thread.

39 b   Layout

Use 8½-by-11-inch paper that is heavy enough to prevent type on the next page from showing through. Use an inkjet or laser printer.

Set page **margins** at one inch at the top, bottom, and sides of body text. **Double-space** all text unless instructed otherwise.

If the **title page** is also the first page of your paper, put your name, your instructor's name, the course title, and the paper's due date at the top left-hand corner, each on a separate, double-spaced line using your regular typeface. Don't indent.

On the next line, center the title of the paper. Use a typeface slightly larger than your body type. Don't underline or italicize your title or put it in quotation marks. Capitalize according to the rules in 68c. On the next line, begin the body of text. (For an example, see Chapter 27.)

If your instructor asks for a separate title page, follow his or her guidelines or those of your discipline. (See Chapter 30.)

Rules for Indenting and Spacing

- Indent the first word of each paragraph five spaces.

- Space once after end punctuation, commas, semi-colons, and colons.

- Do not space between words and quotation marks, parentheses, or brackets (see Chapters 65 and 66).

- Do not space between quotation marks and end punctuation or between double and single quotation marks (see 65a).

- Do not space after a hyphen except in a suspended construction. *The rest of the staff are half- and quarter-time employees* (see 69b–d).

- Do not space on either side of a dash. *Only two players remained—Jordan and Mario* (see 66b).

- Space before and after a slash only when it separates lines of poetry (see 66e).

- To display quotations of more than four typed lines, use block format (see 65a).

In the upper right-hand corner of each manuscript page, put your last name or an abbreviated title followed by the page number, separated by a single space. Do not use slashes, parentheses, periods, the abbreviation *p.,* or the word *page.*

39 c Typography

A **type font** consists of a style of type, or **type face,** in various sizes with variations such as **bold** and *italic.* A **serif font**—like this one—has little strokes at the ends of each letterform. A **sans serif font** consists of type without serifs. Use serif type for body text, as it is easier to read. Use sans serif type for headings, captions, and labels.

For body text, pick a serif font such as Times Roman, Palatino, or New Century Schoolbook, unless your instructor specifies a typewriter-style font, such as Courier. Avoid unusual fonts. Choose a **point size** that is easy to read, usually 10 or 12 points.

```
12 point Courier (serif,
fixed spacing)
```

12 point New Century Schoolbook (serif, proportional spacing)

12 point News Gothic (sans serif, proportional)

Titles and Headings

After selecting the body type, pick a typeface for your title and for headings.

Designing Documents

(Chapter title, 16 pt. Century Gothic bold)

Tools for designing

(First-level heading, 12 pt. Century Gothic bold.)

Typography

(Second-level heading, 12 pt. News Gothic)

Lists and tables

(Third-level heading, 12 pt. Times New Roman bold)

An effective way to introduce a new section is to use a large **initial capital.** This is a capital letter several sizes larger than body type, with the text flowing around it. In Microsoft Word, click Format, Drop Cap, and choose style and size.

Justified or Ragged?

Your word processor can set type **ragged-right,** with an uneven right margin like this, or **justified,** with even margins on both sides, like the body text of this book. Justified type is easier to read than ragged-right type. Make sure, however, that the computer does not leave large spaces between words, especially on short lines. Also check hyphenation. If your word processor makes many hyphenation errors, turn off hyphenation and hyphenate manually.

39 d   Lists and tables

A list of related items needs only a few simple typesetting techniques.

- Indent to distinguish from body type.
- Make all elements parallel in grammatical form.
- Use letters, numbers, or typographical element to introduce each item.

Most word processors can format lists automatically with bullets or numbers.

DESIGN YOUR DOCUMENT	CHECKLIST
1. Set page margins	■ Instructor's preferences
2. Set line spacing	■ Title page elements
3. Select type fonts	■ Page numbering
4. Set style for headings	■ Graphics, illustrations

A **table** can make numbers easier to understand. For a simple series of numbers, set up a table by using tab stops.

Median Income by Age of Householder

15–24	25–34	35–44	45–54	55–64	65+
$27,689	44,473	53,240	58,218	44,992	23,048

Source: 2000 Census

To compare more than one series of numbers, use tab stops or your word processor's table function. Place the table near the text it illustrates.

Median Income by Age, 1993–2000

	1993	1999	2000
15–24	$22,740	26,017	27,689
25–34	36,793	43,591	44,473
35–44	48,063	52,582	53,240
45–54	54,350	58,829	58,218
55–64	39,373	46,095	44,992
65+	20,879	23,578	23,048

Source: 2000 Census

39 e Graphics

The term **graphics** refers to ways of presenting information in nonverbal form, including charts, graphs, and illustrations.

A **line graph,** sometimes called a **fever graph,** can make data easy to see.

A **bar graph** can compare multiple sets of data. Compare this one to its source table in 40d. Which is easier to interpret?

A **pie chart** translates proportions into sections of a circle to compare parts to the whole.

A spreadsheet program can create graphs like these. Enter the underlying data, pick the type of chart, give it a

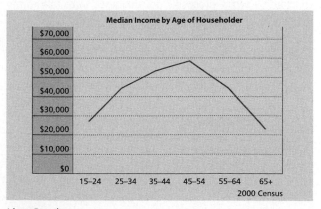

Line Graph

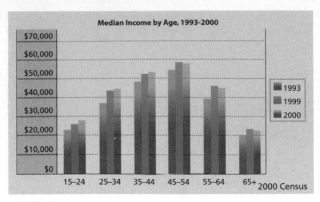

Bar Graph

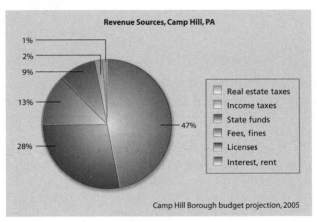

Pie Chart

title, and decide how you want it to appear. Then copy the chart into a word-processor document. Be sure to identify the source of the data.

Use **color** for a specific reason, not just for its own sake. Color can convey information, as it does in a photograph. The colors in the bar graph and pie chart in this section distinguish elements and link them with their descriptions.

39 f Illustrations

Use illustrations not for decoration but to make information easier to understand. A stock photograph—"We followed a trail that looked something like this"—is less effective than a photo that relates specifically to your writing—"We followed Queen's Garden Trail through Bryce Canyon."

Queen's Garden Trail, Bryce Canyon

Mounting a photographic print or a drawing on a page is also acceptable. If you use an image you did not create, be sure to obtain permission and give credit.

WRITING ACROSS THE CURRICULUM

Designing Documents for Specific Audiences

With the help of a librarian or a professor, find papers, newsletters, or Web pages produced by students and professionals in at least two different academic disciplines. What design similarities appear across the disciplines? Within each discipline? What differences appear across disciplines? Pick a document you find visually appealing and effective. Describe the major elements and how they contribute to communicating the author's message.

40 | Internet Writing

Whether you discuss issues on an e-mail list or create a Web page, writing is a big part of the Internet. Your audience will differ in each situation, and each format enables different interactions with other Internet users. You'll write with a primary audience in mind, but there's a secondary audience to consider too—people who happen upon your writings and might need more context or explanation.

40 a   Web audiences

Web audiences read differently from print readers. They scan rather than read deeply. They skip from section to section, page to page, or site to site, looking for items that spark their interest. Others are seeking specific information. If they don't find it quickly, they move on. If they think they might find what they need, they stick around a little longer. If they do find useful information, they linger.

A 2000 study by Stanford University and the Poynter Institute (a newspaper-industry think tank) found that many Web readers focus first on words—headlines, captions, or stories. If the following ideas sound like design issues rather than writing strategies, that's because the Web makes the connections among organization, design, and writing even more important.

On the first page, readers should be able to find the following information, or links to it:

Subject—what's the site about?

Authorship—whose work is this?

Purpose—why was it created?

Contents—beyond the home page, what other content is available?

Context—is there information for readers new to the topic?

Organization—are there links to major sections? How does the reader navigate the site?

Paths—where did the information come from? Where can readers learn more?

Date—when was the site created and last modified?

40 b   Manageable chunks

Don't make readers scroll through long screens; break information into manageable chunks. Create separate pages for background information, answers to common questions, and your reason for creating the site.

Lists make information accessible. Concise writing saves time. Compare the following examples.

MISSION

The Chicago Opera Theater was founded in 1974. The mission of the Theater is to provide first-class productions, drawing from the operatic repertoire of some of the greatest works of the 17th, 18th, and 20th centuries. The Theater aims to produce intimate and innovative performances that are accessible to everyone and to discover and assist the development of the most talented young artists in the United States. The Theater further intends to make itself an integral part of the cultural landscape of Chicago.

MISSION

Founded in 1974, the Chicago Opera Theater's mission is

- To provide first-class productions of operatic repertoire, including the greatest works of the 17th, 18th, and 20th centuries.

- To produce intimate and innovative performances that are accessible to everyone.

- To discover and develop the most talented young artists in the United States.

- To become an integral part of Chicago's cultural landscape.

Both examples contain the same information, but the second, which is what the opera company actually wrote, is easier to read and remember. This works in print, too!

40 c   Nonlinear writing

Breaking information into chunks gives readers a choice of routes. They can read background information first or jump to your conclusions. They can examine your sources or look first at illustrations. But you must *anticipate* these moves and create paths for them.

Suppose you're writing for a history class about the roots of the Civil War. The Whig Party and the Compromise of 1850 will be familiar to your professor and classmates, but other readers will need more background. To find an organization pattern, make a cluster diagram of main ideas.

Grouping and expanding these elements begins to suggest how a Web presentation of your research could be structured, a page or more for each section. These groupings will become the major elements of your presentation. You can use an embellished cluster diagram, like the one

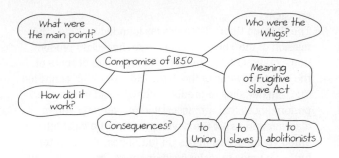

below, or outline each major element on a page of its own, arranged into sequence to create what is called a "story-board" presentation.

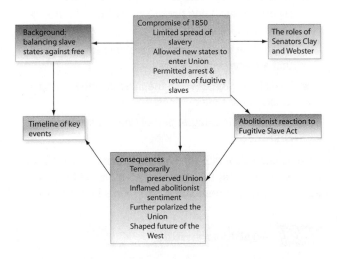

40 d   Links and navigation tools

Once you map the structure, you can begin to imagine the paths readers will need between sections. For example, a main reference to the Fugitive Slave Act should link to its impact among abolitionists. If you have a preferred se-quence in mind, use a *next* link to connect each chunk to the next.

A **navigation bar** is a set of links providing access to all pages in a site. Each page should include a link to other pages in its section, to other sections, and to the home page, so readers can see where they are at all times. Nav-igation links for the Compromise of 1850 paper might look like this.

40 e Resources for Web site builders

Online tutorials can help you get you started building Web sites. Online, check out W3Schools HTML Tutorial http://www.w3schools.com/html/ or search on "HTML tutorial." In print, try *HTML 4 for the World Wide Web* by Elizabeth Castro (Peachpit Press, Berkeley, 2000).

40 f E-mail

In research, e-mail can be a valuable tool, enabling you to ask questions of authors or fellow scholars. Here are a few rules for business and academic e-mail, some learned by painful experience.

1. In academic or business e-mail, write more formally than you would when corresponding with friends.

2. Capitalize appropriately and spell conventionally: *great,* not *gr8.*

3. Avoid instant-messaging style abbreviations such as IMHO (in my humble opinion) or ROFL (rolling on the floor laughing).

4. Limit your use of emoticons to the originals, ? and !

5. E-mail magnifies emotion. If you're angry, draft offline, cool off, and revise before you send.

6. If you have something negative to say—"Your answers seem to contradict one another. Why?"—make contact in person or by phone so that you can modulate your voice and not sound hostile.

7. E-mail is forever. You can't delete all copies, so think before you send.

8. Keep copies. E-mail messages also can vanish. To document an e-mail exchange, save and print copies that include dates and headers.

9. Keep it simple. Many people will recognize and answer only one or two questions per e-mail. If you have more complicated questions, use e-mail to schedule an interview.

WRITING ACROSS THE CURRICULUM

Writing Across the Internet

Pick a Web site that you have found useful for research. How is it organized? What did you notice first? What would you do to improve the site's usefulness for visitors like you?

For a class other than your writing class, find a related e-mail list or newsgroup. Search the archives or current posts for information related to what you're studying. Compare the writing to the materials you've read in that class. What are the similarities and differences? How would you explain them?

41 | *Résumés*

Your résumé summarizes your qualifications for employment. It outlines education, work experience, activities, and interests so that a prospective employer can decide quickly whether you are a good match for a particular job.

If you're applying for a specific position, read the job description. If it isn't included in a posting or an advertisement, call and ask about it. Tailor your résumé by emphasizing the experience that best fits the job description.

A résumé is usually sent out with a cover letter in which you identify yourself, indicate the position you're seeking, and offer additional information that cannot be accommodated on the résumé itself. Keep your résumé brief, preferably no more than one page long, unless you have extensive, relevant experience. Formats vary, but most include the following information:

Personal information Begin with your name, address, and phone numbers, usually centered at the top. Include your e-mail address.

Objective Summarize your objective by naming a specific job or describing a goal: *A position in sports marketing.*

Education List your educational background first only if your relevant work history is limited. Name the last two or three schools you attended (including dates of attendance and degrees), starting with the most recent. Indicate major areas of study. If your grade point average is high, list it. If you've received awards, list them. A résumé is not the place to be modest.

Work experience List all relevant jobs, most recent first, including dates of employment, company name, and a brief description of responsibilities or achievements.

Special skills Mention skills, interests, or activities that provide clues about your abilities and personality, especially if they are relevant to the job in question.

References End with "References available upon request" or provide the names, addresses, and phone numbers of two or three people—teachers, supervisors, employers—whom you trust to give a good reference for you. (Make sure to get their permission first.)

The advantage of the first method is that the employer must indicate an interest in you by contacting you about references, which lets you know where you stand. The advantage of the second is that employers have all the necessary information in one package to make a decision about interviewing you.

Cover letter Write a business letter, addressed by name to the interviewer or decision maker, pointing out features of special interest on your résumé or elaborating upon experience and interest for which there is no room on the résumé proper. Repeat your contact information at the end of the letter.

The two sample résumés that follow contain essentially the same information. The **traditional résumé,** which emphasizes employment history much as outlined above, would be appropriate for applying to any position. The **skills résumé** emphasizes capabilities that would be advantageous if your experience is limited or if you have skills that might be of interest to a particular employer.

I"

Chris Alejandro

PRESENT ADDRESS
405 Martin Street
Lexington, KY 40508
(606) 555-4033
calejandr@magic.uk.edu

PERMANENT ADDRESS
12 Rostow Road
Milwaukee, WI 53713
(414) 555-3421

OBJECTIVE

Internship in arts administration

EDUCATION

BA, University of Kentucky
(expected May 2008)
Major: Business
Minor: Art History
Grade point average: 3.47

I"

AWARDS, HONORS

Martin Perry Scholarship for
Outstanding Business Major;
Honors, School of Business

EMPLOYMENT
2005–2007

Habitat for Humanity: Cochaired
campus fundraising drive that
raised $55,000.

2004–2005

Community Concerts, Inc:
Served as part-time promotion
assistant, handling scheduling,
publicity, subscription procedures,
and fundraising.

2003–2004

Art in the Schools Program
Volunteer, through the Education
Division of the Lexington Center
for the Arts: Trained to conduct
art appreciation presentations
in grade school classrooms,
visiting one school a month.

2001–2003

Music City (part-time and
summers): Worked as sales clerk
and assistant manager.

SPECIAL SKILLS

Word, PowerPoint, Excel,
Web page design

REFERENCES

Available on request

I"

Sample Traditional Résumé

Susan Anderson

Current address

222 Summit Street
Burlington, VT 05401

(802) 555-1234
susan.anderson@uvm.edu

Telephone and e-mail

OBJECTIVE: Researcher/writer for nonprofit environmental organization.

EDUCATION

University of Vermont, School of Natural Resources, Geology and English double major. GPA: 3.6. Expected graduation, May 2008.

Fairfield High School, Fairfield, OH. 1999–2003. Activities included debate team, Spanish Club, student newspaper, field hockey, swimming.

SKILLS

Field research. Extensive experience analyzing natural plant communities, quantifying data, surveying field sites, and drawing topographical site maps.

Computer literacy. Fluent in MS Word, Excel, PowerPoint, Adobe Premier, Sigmaplot, INFORM, QuarkXPress.

Spanish. Fluent after four years of secondary and college study, including AFS summer abroad in Quito, Ecuador.

RELEVANT ENVIRONMENTAL COURSEWORK

Field Ecology Methods
Fundamentals of Field Science
Landscape Inventory and Assessment
Nature Writing

RESEARCH EXPERIENCE

Southwest Earth Studies, June–August 2006. Internship to research acid mine drainage in the San Juan Mountains, CO; grant, National Science Foundation.

Field Research of the Newark Rift Basin, June 2005. Internship to study water flow in Newark, NJ, rift basin; Newark Environment Foundation Fellowship.

COMMUNICATIONS EXPERIENCE

Editorial Assistant, *Wild Gulf Journal,* Chewonki Foundation, January 2005–December 2006. Edited 70-page quarterly journal of environmental education resources for the Lake Champlain watershed.

Tutor, Writing Center, University of Vermont, September 2004–December 2005. Counseled students on papers for introductory geology courses.

LEADERSHIP EXPERIENCE

English Majors' Student Representative, University of Vermont, September 2004–May 2005. Elected to represent 200 English majors and participate as a voting member at faculty meetings and on curriculum revision committee.

Local Foods Coordinator, Onion River Coorperative, Burlington, VT, January 2004–May 2005. Ordered produce and coordinated pickups from local farms.

REFERENCES: Available on request

Sample Skills Résumé

42 | *Oral Presentations*

Public speaking is another way of "publishing" ideas that originate in written form. In speaking, as in writing, it's important to present ideas with confidence, clarity, accuracy, and grace.

42 a   The assignment

Identify your purpose. Are you presenting information, raising questions, arguing a position, or leading a class activity? You'll need to believe in and understand your subject.

Know your audience. In most class settings, your audience comprises your instructor and classmates. To keep them interested, present something they don't already know, building on issues or ideas raised in class.

Collaborate. In a group project,

1. Agree on what your task entails.
2. Divide tasks equitably; do your part promptly, and hold others accountable for theirs.
3. Plan who will report what and for how long.

42 b   Preparing a speaking text

Writing a speech follows the same process as other kinds of writing.

Research. Find text sources; talk to experts; conduct surveys; visit sites.

Invent. Allow time to think, plan, invent, discover—don't try to prepare your whole text the night before it is due.

Compose. Even if you don't intend to read it out loud, write out your report and read it aloud. Edit for ease of reading, and be sure your presentation fits the allotted time.

Outline. Effective oral reports are spoken, not read, with the speaker making eye contact with the audience. Thus the "final draft" of an oral report is a "speaking outline" or notes to be glanced at as needed.

Prepare note cards. In a brief report, a one-page outline will be enough. For longer reports, use index cards, which are easier to handle.

Start strong. To get everyone listening, speakers commonly use questions, stories, or jokes. Be sure any story or joke you tell is relevant.

Write simply. Avoid jargon, and explain key concepts.

Repeat key points. The old advice to speakers is "Tell what you're gonna tell 'em. Tell 'em. Then tell 'em what you've told 'em." Repetition helps listeners understand.

Create listening signposts. Tell listeners what's coming. For example, tell your audience you are going to make three points, then list them.

Finish strong. Be sure that when time is up, you've stated your conclusion clearly.

42 c Speaking in public

Unless you're a veteran speaker, nervousness is unavoidable; accept it, and try to harness its energy.

Rehearse. Running through your talk out loud several times will help you understand your material better. Make an audio or video recording, or practice in front of a mirror.

Make the room your own. Set up the room to suit your presentation. Rearrange things if necessary. If you don't plan to use a lectern, move it to one side. If you use the lectern, stand still and rest your hands on it. If you prefer your audience in a semicircle or in groups instead of straight rows, set up the chairs in advance, or ask them to move closer.

Leave time for questions. When giving oral reports, it is customary to allow your audience time to ask questions. Plan for this time, show your willingness to discuss further what you know, and always answer succinctly and honestly; if you don't know an answer, say so.

42 d   Creative options

Here are some ideas for enhancing your presentation:

Handouts. If you want listeners to retain information, put it in their hands. Be sure to make enough for everyone.

Use *prepared* visual aids such as videos, films, maps, charts, sketches, photographs, posters, computer graphics, or projected transparencies. With computer programs such as *PowerPoint (see the box below)*, it is easy to prepare professional-quality visual aids.

Use *process* visual aids to illustrate something in front of your audience. If you plan to write on a blackboard or a flip chart, bring chalk or markers.

Use audio aids. Audience attention picks up noticeably when you introduce sounds or voices other than your own.

***Be* an audio-visual aid.** If a live demonstration is appropriate, be sure to have the equipment you need.

Ask your audience to write. For example, on the subject of "alcohol on campus," ask people to jot down their own thoughts, telling them their notes will remain private. Then ask them to share—not read—their ideas with a neighbor for a few minutes. The conversation will pull them in further, and the buzz in the room makes everyone—especially you—more comfortable. To resume control, ask for volunteer opinions and use these as a bridge to your presentation.

WRITING ACROSS THE CURRICULUM

Guidelines for PowerPoint Presentations

Across the curriculum, PowerPoint has become the standard visual aid program for presentations. With a computer projector, it allows you to show text, slides, graphics, photos, and moving images to supplement oral presentations in any course of study. The following tips will help you create an effective presentation and avoid both cuteness and clichés.

- **Prepare good material.** No slick slide show can enhance shallow ideas: do your homework, and back up claims with evidence.

- **Keep it simple.** Follow an outline, using slides to highlight major points. Fill-in details orally, by careful explanation, not by reading the material on your slides.

- **Make organization visible.** If your outline has three sections, consider starting with a slide listing points I, II, and III. Then show the main points of Section I in one or more slides, followed by the main points of Section II, and so on.

- **Check** lighting and sight lines. Make sure the room can be darkened and that the screen isn't facing the light. Make sure the whole audience can see the screen.

- **Estimate the distance** from the farthest seat to the screen. Use the sign-painter's rule: one-inch letters can be read from ten feet, two-inch letters from twenty feet, and so on. Adjust type accordingly. (On a monitor, 72-point type is about one inch high.)

- **Consider readability** when choosing colors for background and type. Complementary colors (e.g., red on green) may be hard to see; other combinations (e.g., black on yellow) may need to be toned down. Choose light colors for backgrounds.

- **Use art carefully.** If a photo or graphic is the best way to convey information, use it. Most clip art figures look amateurish.

- **Avoid unnecessary animation.** Moving type, elements that fade into or out of view, and animated graphics can distract from what you're saying.

- **Rehearse** with a tape recorder and a computer so you can watch and listen to your presentation at the same time.

A CAUTION ABOUT *POWERPOINT*

Slide programs such as PowerPoint can have a downside, causing presenters to oversimplify their material, present too many glitzy slides, and read from the screen rather than speak directly to listeners. (For more on the pitfalls of presentation software, see "PowerPoint is Evil" by Edward Tufte http://www.wired.com/wired/archive/11.09/ppt2.html.)

PART nine

Editing for Clarity

Careful editing answers the following questions:

- Does my introduction catch the reader's attention? (Chapter 44)
- Is my main point (or thesis) clearly stated? (Chapter 13)
- Does my conclusion produce the right effect? (Chapter 45)
- Does one paragraph lead logically to the next? (Chapter 43)
- Are my sentences interesting and varied? (Chapter 46)
- Are my sentences clear, direct, and economical? (Chapters 46–49)
- Is my language matched to my audience? (Chapters 50–51)

By asking these questions in specific situations, you will generate alternative solutions and choose among them. That process is called editing.

43 *Effective Paragraphs*

G ood paragraphing groups related sentences together to help readers follow the author's ideas. When a new paragraph begins, readers expect a new idea or direction to begin. They expect that within a paragraph, each sentence will help develop or advance a main idea—that the paragraph will be **unified.** Readers also expect that each paragraph will present its ideas in an order that makes sense—that it will be **organized.** And they expect that each sentence within a paragraph will relate clearly to the sentences around it—that it will be **coherent.**

43 a Unity

To edit for unity, determine the paragraph's main idea or topic. Keep words or sentences that clarify that main idea, and delete or move those that do not. A **topic sentence** states the key idea clearly and helps readers follow an argument. In experiential or reflective writing, paragraph topics are more often implied than stated, but you should check to see that they are clear.

In the following passage, the writer identified the first sentence as her topic sentence but realized that her fourth sentence did not illustrate the topic sentence. She moved it to the next paragraph, where it fit better.

For various reasons, some unhappy couples remain married. Some are forbidden to divorce by religion, others by social custom. Still others stay together "for the sake of the children." In recent years, psychologists and sociologists have studied families to determine whether more harm is done to children by divorce or by parents who stay together despite conflict. ~~But by staying together, such parents feel~~ *believing* they are sparing their children the pain of divorce.

In his study of family conflict, Robert S. Weiss found that children in such families were often happiest "when Daddy is at work."

43 b   Organization

Within paragraphs, try to organize sentences according to a clear pattern. Which pattern you choose depends on what you are trying to do. The following patterns are familiar, so readers will follow them easily, but many other organizing ideas would work as well.

General to specific. Begin with a general statement (often this is the *topic sentence* of your paragraph) and provide examples. For example, start with a statement about kitchens; then move to what's in them—stoves, refrigerators, toasters, and so on. A clear topic sentence followed by examples is easy to follow.

Specific to general. Start with a series of details that lead to a general statement: Describe the stoves, toasters, and refrigerators; then show how they add up to a kitchen. Placing your general statement at the end emphasizes the larger category.

Chronological. Present events in the order in which they happened: *first the fog, then the rain, finally the sun.* The topic sentence, or general statement, can appear at the beginning or the end of the paragraph.

Reverse chronological. Move backward from the most recent events to the most distant: *today, last week, a year ago.* It is an effective way to reflect on the past.

Climactic order. Use suspense to build toward a conclusion: *begin with confusion, follow with difficulties, conclude with victory.*

Spatial. Lead the viewer's eye from one object to another, ending where something happens: *first the door, then the window, then the chair, finally the note on the table.*

Your word processor can help you generate alternatives: (1) Insert returns so that each sentence begins on a new line, and then rearrange sentences until you find the best organization. (2) Use the copy function to make several copies of the same paragraph; organize each in a different way, and compare and choose the best one for your situation.

43 c Coherence

A paragraph coheres—"sticks together"—when each of its sentences relates appropriately to the surrounding ones. Use *transitional expressions* (e.g., *however, furthermore, at the same time, meanwhile*) to signal to readers that you are comparing or contrasting ideas, showing relationships in time and space, suggesting cause and effect, and so on. In this paper on divorce, the writer added a transitional sentence to mark a change in the direction of her argument.

> During a divorce, parents have the ability to shield a child from potential harm. Many couples who stay together believe that the two-parent structure is crucial to the child's well-being. *This, however, appears not to be the case.* Judith Wallerstein finds that a stable, caring relationship between a child and each parent indvidually is the most significant ingredient in a child's emotional health (143). Maintaining even one stable relationship appears to reduce the effect of divorce on a child's emotions.

Without the added sentence, the reader might not understand the significance of the Wallerstein quotation.

Here are some other strategies to ensure coherence:

Break long paragraphs. Find divisions suggested by the content. Be sure shorter paragraphs retain enough content to make sense.

Connect short paragraphs. Look for places where paragraphs can be combined into more substantial ones, or develop the short ones with further information.

Repeat key words. Selectively repeating key words is another cohering device that makes it easier for readers to follow your thoughts.

Move from familiar to new. Within each sentence and each paragraph, refer first to concepts already established, and build toward the unfamiliar.

44 | *Strong Openings*

The first words of your paper may be the most important. Your opening must engage your readers, introduce your topic and your main idea, and point toward what you intend to say. In a short two- or three-page essay, one paragraph may suffice to open. In longer papers, you may have a page or two to play with. Here are some techniques for making openings more engaging:

Build toward a thesis statement: Start by identifying a topic, and progress toward a statement that you will attempt to prove.

> When the National Hockey League lockout canceled the 2004–2005 season, sports cable networks scrambled for new programming. They discovered to their surprise people would watch televised poker games. With card games drawing more viewers than ice hockey and professional soccer continuing to struggle for an audience, the nation is ready for a new sports craze. Lacrosse is the television sport of the future.

Open with a striking assertion: Make a statement so bold or far-reaching that the reader will demand to see your evidence.

> Slam dunks are rare, and offensive schemes depend on ball movement. The pick and roll lives. Players remember to box out when rebounding. A basketball purist watching a WNBA game might conclude that, inch for inch, women play the game better than men.

Open with an anecdote: Tell a brief story that introduces the topic and illustrates the thesis.

> When Jenny Wilkins was ten years old, she was barely five feet tall. But her skillful handling of a basketball brought her to the attention of a prep school coach who changed Jenny's life as she has changed the lives of dozens of other student athletes.

Open with an interesting detail, statistic, or quotation: Plunge readers into an unfamiliar situation to pique their curiosity.

> Through the cockpit window I could see the other plane approaching. It grew from a dot to a silvery blur that closed at nearly 600 mph. As it roared past barely one thousand feet overhead, the blast of its engine shook the deck beneath us.

Open with a provocative question: Pose the question that your thesis will answer.

> The thought of them might make your skin crawl, and their bites might make you itch. Perhaps you spray chemicals around your house to kill them. But have you ever wondered what the world would be like without insects?

Edit every sentence: Rewrite first-draft openings to eliminate unnecessary words, empty phrases, and clichés—all of which make for dull reading.

> it is a fact that, it is interesting to note that, first and foremost, last but not least

45 | Thoughtful Closings

I f readers could remember only one paragraph of your essay, what would you want it to say? That's your conclusion, a closing paragraph that lingers with readers, making the strongest statement of your case that you can support. Here are some techniques:

Close with a rhetorical question. Such a question is not to be answered but to persuade the reader to agree with you:

> How can concerned citizens stand by and do nothing?

Close with a genuine question. Acknowledge that you don't have all the answers:

> What will happen to the American economy when the oil reserves are gone?

Close with a call to action. Use your powers of persuasion to mobilize readers to action:

> It's time for all of us to eat more carefully, walk more deliberately, and slow down.

Close with a prediction. Imagine the future if the action you propose is—or is not—taken:

> If we don't stop motorists from talking on cell phones, such accidents will continue.

46 Sentence Variety

A passage consisting of many sentences of the same type and length can be tedious. Moreover, unless you make it clear how each sentence relates to the next, a passage can be confusing. Combining sentences can keep readers moving and show how ideas relate logically. First, a reminder about sentence types.

A simple sentence has a single **independent clause**—at least a subject and a verb, more commonly a subject, verb, and object.

>   s   v
> Smoke rises.
>   s   v   o
> Pollution endangers public health.

Two or more independent clauses can be joined into one sentence using either a comma and a coordinating conjunction or using a semicolon. The result is called a **compound sentence.**

> Pollution is a problem, and it won't go away soon.
>
> Recycling will help; it saves on landfill space.

Two sentences can be joined into one by making one the main clause and the other a **dependent clause.** A clause that begins with a word such as *when, because, that, which,* or *since* is called a dependent clause because it makes no sense by itself; it has to be part of a larger sentence.

>   dependent clause
> Because the problem continues to grow,
>   independent clause
> legislators must act before it is too late.

Sentences can have more than one of either kind of clause.

independent clause   independent clause
Pollution can be prevented, and we must take
                                    dependent clause
action to stop it because there is no other way to

survive on this planet.

Using *coordination, subordination,* and *parallel structure* can help you show connections between ideas.

46 a   Coordination

If two sentences have equal importance and related meaning, consider combining them into a compound sentence using one of the coordinating conjunctions: *for, and, nor, but, or, yet, so.*

We had eggs for breakfast, and then we went for a walk.

Avoid using coordination where the meaning of the two sentences is not related closely enough to warrant joining them:

I made eggs for breakfast, and I missed the bus.

46 b   Subordination

In the following simple sentences, two ideas are presented as roughly equal:

John Playford collected seventeenth-century music. He was an English musician.

You can emphasize one idea by subordinating the other.

John Playford, an English musician, collected seventeenth-century music.
(emphasizes his activity)

John Playford, who collected seventeenth-century music, was an English musician.
(emphasizes his identity)

46 c Parallel structures

Repeating a grammatical structure within a sentence is called **parallelism,** a technique that can highlight a comparison. In the following examples, parallelism creates a pleasing rhythm.

WORDS

We saw the children swimming, jumping, and splashing.

PHRASES

Of the people, by the people, for the people.

CLAUSES

Where there's smoke, there's fire.

Repetition and rhythm make parallel constructions powerful and memorable. Instead of settling for *"Laura likes painting and writing, and she likes to read,"* make the second construction match the first: *"Laura likes painting, writing, and reading."*

Instead of *"Wind power is difficult to capture, and it costs a lot to store,"* write *"Wind power is not only difficult to capture but expensive to store."*

47 | Concise Sentences

A cademic, business, and technical writing should convey information clearly, to help the reader understand without undue effort. Edit to express ideas with few wasted words.

47 a Generalities

Sometimes writers make statements that are vague to the point of being meaningless: *It is our duty today to take responsibility for our actions.* (When was it not so?) At other times a generality is so widely accepted that stating it seems silly: *Shakespeare is a great writer.* (Yes?)

Some generalities indulge in circular reasoning: *During the harsh winters of the 1870s, the weather was very cold.* (*Harsh* implies that.) Others announce that a point is going to be made but don't make it: *Many factors played a part in the Bush victory.* (What factors?)

Although generalities can appear anywhere, look particularly at openings and conclusions, where you may be trying hard to impress. Look for the obvious and edit it out:

Fetal alcohol syndrome affects one of every 750

newborn babies, ~~It is clearly not good for them,~~

causing coordination problems, malformed organs,

small brains, short attention spans, and behavioral

problems.

47 b   Idle words

Speakers use seemingly unnecessary words when they talk, sometimes to ensure understanding. Writers of first drafts similarly digress on their way to finding out what they really want to say, more precisely, in a subsequent draft.

To edit ~~very~~ wordy drafts, test each ~~and every~~ word

to see if eliminating it ~~tightens the expression and~~

~~makes it more concise or~~ changes the meaning. If *not,*

~~the meaning is ultimately unchanged, consider~~

cut~~ting~~ it.

47 c   Automatic phrases

Phrases like *in my opinion, it has come to my attention that,* and *due to the fact that* contribute nothing. They are "throat clearing," appearing at the beginnings of sentences or wherever a writer is grasping for reinforcement. When you find an automatic phrase, remove it and reread the passage. If no meaning is lost, leave it out. If some meaning seems to be missing, try condensing the phrase.

Today   often

~~In this day and age~~ children ~~in many instances~~
know more about black holes than they do about
seashells.

47 d Wordy phrases

Vague nouns—*area, aspect, factor, kind, manner, nature,
tendency, thing,* and *type*—can create wordiness. Often you
can delete imprecise phrases, condense them, or find more
concrete substitutes. If you have written *"One of the factors
that gave them problems in the lab was the tendency toward contamination,"* be more direct: *"Contamination was
a problem in the lab"* or *"The lab was contaminated."*

47 e Useless modifiers

Writers often use modifiers such as *clearly, obviously, in-
terestingly, undoubtedly, absolutely, fortunately, hopefully,
really, totally,* and *very* to make a sentence sound forceful
or authoritative. A sentence usually sounds more direct
without them.

These intensifiers ~~clearly~~ add ~~very~~ little, and they
can ~~hopefully~~ be deleted.

47 f Redundancy

Public speakers are often advised, "Tell them what you're
going to say; say it; then tell them what you said." In speaking, repetition helps listeners understand. In writing, however, where readers are able to slow down, reread, and
pause as they please, repetition can be ineffective. Ask
yourself whether each repetition links ideas, sustains an
established rhythm, or prevents confusion. If not, cut it.

The ~~general~~ consensus ~~of opinion~~ among students
was that the chancellor had exceeded her authority.

Consensus means a broadly held opinion.
    If you find yourself repeating the same word or using
a similar one, look for ways to eliminate one of them.

About ninety percent
~~A very high percentage~~ of the prison's inmates take
advantage of the special education program, ~~about ninety percent.~~

47 g Elliptical constructions

By omitting words that readers can be expected to supply
for themselves, an **elliptical construction** helps avoid un-
needed repetition. Such constructions are usually used in
the second part of a parallel construction, where the first
verb is implied for the second as well.

> Her words suggested one thing, her actions
> ~~suggested~~ another.

> Of Shakespeare's female characters, Lady Macbeth
> is the most ruthless; Desdemona the most loving,
> and Portia the most resourceful.

47 h Pretentious language

When you want to sound authoritative, it is tempting to use
technical, obscure, or ornate language. When such language
is needlessly complicated or overinflated, it is called *pretentious*. Pretentious language uses two or three words where
one would do and relies excessively on the passive voice.
Find concrete subjects for your verbs, and address your readers more directly; rewriting is usually in order because cross-
ing out existing language is seldom enough.

PRETENTIOUS
The range of audio-visual services provided
includes examinations to determine optical or
auditory impairment.

CONCISE
We offer eye and ear examinations.

47 i Euphemisms

A *euphemism* is an inoffensive word or phrase deliberately
substituted for one considered harsh or indelicate. Our conversations are full of euphemisms, especially words for

money, death, sex, and body functions. Workers are fired in massive layoffs, but companies call it *downsizing.* A person whose grandmother has died says, "*I lost my grandmother,*" and so on.

In academic writing, you strive to inform, not to obscure, so you must balance your audience's comfort with the need to be clear. If in doubt, ask a peer or an instructor to check your choices.

48 | *Strong Verbs*

Verbs drive sentences the way an engine moves a car. They make the subjects (nouns) of sentences *race, run, erupt, scoot, shoot, dive, fly, climb, sprawl, meander, wonder,* and *ponder* toward one end or another and, in the process, enliven your writing.

48 a   Action verbs

Action verbs—verbs that denote specific actions—make things happen. Verbs that show no action—*be, appear, become, seem, exist*—can leave your sentences underpowered. Replace these **static verbs** with action verbs whenever you can.

> This problem will soon ~~become evident~~ erupt.

A form of *be* preceding a phrase or a clause often signals a stronger verb coming up. Make the stronger verb the main verb of the sentence.

> The most effective writers ~~are those who~~ write as though they were simply talking.

Sentences beginning with *there are, there is,* and *it is* often conceal stronger verbs. In these cases, look for the real main verb of the sentence.

> Many ~~There are many~~ people ~~who~~ believe that Elvis Presley is still alive, even though ~~it is~~ only the tabloids ~~that~~ take such so-called news seriously.

48 b Weak action verbs

Not all verbs that describe action evoke clear images. Overuse has exhausted the image-making power of such verbs as *do, get, go, have, make,* and *think.* As you edit, watch for weak action verbs and substitute stronger verbs where possible.

> *bakes*
> He ~~makes~~ excellent sourdough bread.

A verb that relies on other words for its descriptive power often can be replaced with a stronger one.

> *scurried*
> He ~~walked quickly~~ from the room.

48 c Hidden verbs

Many English verbs have been changed into useful nouns with the help of a suffix—*announce/announcement* or *tempt/temptation,* for example. These **nominalizations** often bury the real action of a sentence, and to make matters worse, they usually require a static verb—*have, do, make,* or *be.* Dig up the buried verbs to resurrect your point.

> *satisfactorily explain*
> Few biographies of FDR ~~have given a satisfactory explanation of~~ the disastrous Yalta conference.

Buried Verbs

Replace these common expressions with the action verbs buried within them.

NOMINAL EXPRESSION	BURIED VERB
put forth a proposal	propose
hold a discussion	discuss
formulate a plan	plan
reach a decision	decide
arrive at a conclusion	conclude
hold a meeting	meet
make a choice	choose

48 d   Active voice

When a verb is in the **active voice,** the person or thing performing the action is the subject, which is the most natural, economical, and direct form of English expression.

actor	active-voice verb	direct object (recipient of action)
Juana	collects	the tickets.

When a verb is in the **passive voice,** the recipient of the action becomes the subject, and there is no object. Passive voice sentences can be harder for readers to unravel.

subject of action	passive-voice verb	agent of action
The photos	were taken	by Juana.

Advantages of the Active Voice

By focusing on the actor, the active voice helps readers visualize what happens and who does it. Active-voice sentences are usually shorter and more direct than passive-voice sentences. (The sentences in this paragraph and the majority throughout this book are in the active voice.)

Advantages of the Passive Voice

The passive voice deemphasizes the actor and highlights the recipient of the verb's action—an effect you may choose for selected occasions such as the following:

TO STRESS RESULTS
A $500 million reduction in the national debt was approved by Congress.

TO LEAVE THE AGENT UNSTATED
The city's first homeless shelter was established in a vacant warehouse.

TO ASSERT OBJECTIVITY
The samples were tested for bacteria.

Disdvantages of the Passive Voice

Do not use the passive voice as a substitute for real objectivity or to avoid placing responsibility.

Mistakes were made.   *By whom?*

49 | *Specific Nouns and Modifiers*

Compare the mental pictures you get from the phrases *an old car* versus *a rusted, baby–blue '75 VW Beetle.* The first phrase evokes the abstract category *cars* but supplies no specific image; the second shows a specific concrete car that readers can visualize. When sentences contain specific identifiable "characters," such as the blue Beetle, they tell small stories that readers can recognize.

Abstract words refer to ideas and concepts that cannot be perceived by the senses: *transportation, wealth, childhood, nutrition.* **Concrete words** name things that can be seen, felt, heard, tasted, or smelled: *a dime, a child, broccoli, cement.*

General words refer to categories and groups: *pets, stores, teachers, cars.* **Specific words** identify individual objects or people: *Rover, Murphy's Drugs, Pauline Clea, the '75 Beetle.*

49 a Concrete nouns

We would be unable to think, speak, and write about *literature, constitutionality,* or *music* without terms for these abstract ideas. However, writing that relies exclusively on abstractions seems like nothing but hot air. To give form and life to the abstract and general, look for specific details and examples to support them.

> Campus radicalism increased in the 1960s and
>   , such as the one at Kent State University in Ohio,
> 1970s. Antiwar demonstrations were common.
>   ^

49 b Specific modifiers

Choose modifiers (words and phrases that describe nouns and verbs) that are specific and concrete. Choose modifiers that appeal to the senses: *red* peppers, *whispered* words, *hot* stove, *sweet* peaches, *oily* skin.

Some descriptive modifiers have become empty and meaningless through overuse. Be wary of *pretty, dull, dumb, nice, beautiful, good, bad, young, old, great, fantastic, terrible, awesome, awful.*

Madeline was a ~~very pretty~~ girl with ~~nice~~ brown eyes.

(edit: "fair-skinned" inserted above "very pretty"; "laughing" inserted above "nice")

50 | *The Right Word*

The English language has a rich vocabulary. The place you live, for instance, might be your *house, home, residence, abode, dwelling, domicile, habitation, quarters, lodging, apartment, pad, place, shack, spot,* or *digs.* It's your job as a writer to find the right word to convey your meaning.

Most writers rely on dictionaries and usage guides to guide them in the use of language. If you consult these books regularly, your word skills and your writing will improve.

50 a   Roots, prefixes, and suffixes

Roots, prefixes, and suffixes provide substantial clues to a word's meaning. A root is a base word, or part of a word, from which other words are formed: *mile* in the word *mileage.*

A **prefix** is a group of letters attached to the beginning of a root that changes its meaning: *un-* in *unfinished.* The word *prefix* itself consists of a root, *-fix,* which means "attach," and a prefix, *pre-,* meaning "before." A **suffix** is a group of letters attached to the end of a root: *-age* in *mileage.*

Both prefixes and suffixes change the meaning of the root to which they are attached. For example, the words *antebellum, bellicose,* and *belligerent* share the root *bellum,* Latin for "war." If you already know that *belligerent* means "warlike or at war," you might guess that *antebellum* means "before war."

50 b   Denotation and connotation

The **denotation** of a word is its direct, literal meaning. *Fragrance, odor,* and *smell* all denote something detected by your olfactory sense. But the associations, or *connotations,* of the words differ. *"You have a distinct fragrance"* suggests a pleasant smell, whereas *"You have a distinct odor"* suggests something else. The associated, or indirect, meaning of a word is its **connotation.** Edit carefully for unintended connotations.

50 c   Idiomatic expressions

Why do we ride *in* a car but *on* a train? Why do we *take* a picture but *make* a recording? Such widely accepted speech patterns are called **idioms,** patterns that may not follow rules of logic or grammar. Prepositions—*at, by, for, in, on, out, to,* etc.—show a relationship between a noun or a pronoun and other words in the sentence. If you are uncertain about whether to trust your ear for standard usage, consult a dictionary or a guide to usage.

50 d   Slang, regionalisms, and colloquialisms

Everyone uses *slang,* informal language that originates in and is unique to small groups such as students, musicians, athletes, or politicians: "Just want to hang with the homeys." Some slang words eventually enter the mainstream and become part of standard English. A *jeep* was originally slang for a general-purpose (g.p.) military vehicle used in World War II. Now it is the brand name of a four-wheel-drive vehicle driven by many Americans.

Regionalisms are expressions used in one part of the country but not common elsewhere. The name for a carbonated beverage, for example, varies by region from *pop* to *soda* to *soft drink* to *seltzer.* Some bits of regional dialect are regarded as nonstandard—that is, not widely used in academic writing.

A *colloquialism* is an expression common to spoken language but seldom used in formal writing: "Can I get you something to drink awhile?" "The barn needs painted."

Use slang, regionalisms, and colloquialisms sparingly in academic writing. They may not be understood, and their informality may imply a lack of rigor on your part. They can, however, convey immediacy and authenticity in descriptions and dialogue.

50 e Jargon

Every profession or field develops terms to express its special ideas. Such specialized or technical language is called *jargon.* As you edit, decide whether all your terminology will be understood by your audience. Using fewer technical terms helps you communicate better with a general audience, but a specialized audience expects you to use technical language appropriately. For example, for what kind of audience would you substitute *femur* for *thigh bone* or vice versa? Avoid jargon added merely to make your writing sound important.

> **ORIGINAL**
> The range of diagnostic audio-visual services provided includes examinations to determine optical or auditory impairment.
>
> **EDITED**
> We offer eye and ear examinations.

50 f Figurative language

Figurative language likens one thing to another in imaginative ways. A **metaphor** describes one thing in terms of another: *The news* rippled *through the crowd.* An **analogy** directly compares one thing to another: *Readers are like bus riders; they like to know where they are being taken.* Skillful metaphors and analogies offer readers ways to envision your ideas.

However, not all images fit together. A **mixed metaphor** combines unrelated images, often with unintended effects. When you find a mixed metaphor, eliminate the weaker one and extend the more appropriate one.

> We must swim against the tide of cynicism that
> threatens to ~~cloud our vision~~ of a world without
>   *drown our hope*
> hunger.

Swim/tide/drown/hope make a more consistent and, therefore, clearer image than *swim/tide/cloud/vision*.

50 g Clichés

Our language is full of overused expressions that no longer conjure images in the reader's mind. Here are some common *clichés*—how many more can you think of?

the last straw	needle in a haystack
sharp as a tack	writing on the wall
lay your cards on the table	toe the line
a drop in the bucket	hit the nail on the head
best thing since sliced bread	jump-start the economy

When you find a cliché in your writing, simply replace it with a direct statement of what you are trying to say.

Editing to correct a cliché is ~~easy as pie.~~
                                               not difficult.

51 *Unbiased Language*

U sing a generalization about a group of people to predict, describe, or interpret the behavior or characteristics of an individual in that group is both insensitive and illogical. Careless generalizations based on race, ethnicity, gender, cultural background, age, physical characteristics, or lifestyles are called *stereotypes*. Whether they refer to gender, race, ethnicity, or sexual preference, stereotypes substitute a simplistic formula for an appreciation of individual differences and the richness of human variation.

51 a Recognizing stereotypes

Many stereotypes stem from ignorance and from fear of people who are perceived as different. These stereotypes penetrate our language in labels for people—*liberal politician*—and in descriptions—*sleepy Southern town*. Calling a doctor or a lawyer *he* reinforces the stereotype that all doctors and lawyers are men.

Edit to eliminate stereotypes. Qualify broad generalizations, and support or replace sweeping statements with specific factual evidence. In some cases, drop the stereotypical observation altogether.

> *inexperienced*
> Like most ~~teenage~~ drivers, he was reckless.
>   ^

> ~~Like so many of his race,~~ Michael Jordan was a superbly gifted athlete.

51 b   Choosing group labels

Labels are sometimes necessary for discussing groups of people. However, labels inevitably emphasize a single aspect of identity, ignoring other characteristics. They also may offend people who do not want to be so characterized. Furthermore, many labels go beyond identification and become explicitly or implicitly derogatory. As you edit, examine any labels you have used; try to use only those acceptable to the members of the group themselves, and avoid labels with negative connotations.

Designations of Race, Ethnicity, and Nationality

The terms *black, African American,* and *people of color* are widely used. Some spokespeople and many of the media have adopted the term *African American* as both an adjective and a noun.

The terms *Asian* and *Asian American* have widely replaced *Oriental,* which to some ears carries a note of condescension. It is always correct to refer to an individual's or group's national origin of ancestry, using a specific country of origin: *Japanese, Korean, Malaysian, Chinese.*

Today, some Americans of Spanish-speaking heritage refer to themselves as *Hispanics;* others prefer *Latino* and *Latina;* and some Mexican Americans, *Chicano* and *Chicana,* which refer explicitly to Mexican origins. Many *Native Americans* prefer that term to *Indian,* but using the name of the tribe or nation is often a better choice: *Navajo, Lakota Sioux, Seneca.* Some *Inuit* prefer that term to *Eskimo.*

Designations of Gender and Sexual Orientation

Most adult women prefer to be called *women* rather than *girls* or *ladies. Girls* is particularly inappropriate in reference to salespeople, administrative staff, or those in service jobs.

When writing about sexual orientation, keep in mind that people have widely different views about the role of sexuality in our personal and public lives. Be aware that not everyone may share your perspective, and consider using a group's own chosen term.

Designations of Ability

People with physical limitations often prefer *disabled* to *handicapped.* The phrase *uses a wheelchair* is preferable to *confined to a wheelchair.*

Designations of Age

Modern American culture does not extol old age, and even accepted terms can describe it bluntly or condescendingly. If a person's age is critical to what you want to say, cite the person's actual age: 68-year-old skier.

Checking Labels for Negative Connotations

Some labels that seem neutral hide negative connotations. For example, the term *AIDS victims* implies the people in question are blameless, which you may intend, but also that they are helpless, which you may not. *People with AIDS* is preferable.

51 c Using gender-neutral language

When you use words that embody sexual stereotypes, you run the risk of alienating half—or more—of your potential audience. The appearance of gender bias can arise from unexamined habits of thought and language.

Pronoun Choice

Until recently, *he, him,* and *his* were used generically to refer to singular nouns or pronouns whose gender was unknown, unstated, or irrelevant: *Anyone who believes those promises should have his head examined.* Such usage is disappearing because the generic *he* appears to exclude women.

However, English does not have a singular personal pronoun that doesn't specify gender, as *they* does in the plural. In speaking, people often use plural pronouns to avoid the masculine forms: *Everyone had fun on their vacations.* But any pronoun that refers to *everyone* must be singular, so *their* is incorrect.

If you know the gender of the first reference, the solution is simple: *Each nun makes her own bed.* If you don't know the gender, choose one of these strategies:

1. Make the antecedent plural and adjust other agreement problems:

   All the residents make ~~Everyone makes~~ their own ~~bed.~~ *beds.*

2. Use *his or her:*

   Each resident makes ~~their~~ *his or her* own bed.

3. Restructure the sentence:

   Everyone has ~~done his part.~~ *helped.*

Universal Terms

The terms *man* and *mankind* seem to ignore the female half of the species. As you edit, substitute inclusive terms such as *humanity, the human race, humankind,* or *people.*

Occupational Terms

In choosing terms for occupation, focus on the occupation, not the gender of the person who holds it. Almost no jobs are "naturally" held exclusively by men or women. Avoid language that implicitly identifies an occupation with gender by implying that all flight attendants, nurses, secretaries, or teachers are female or assuming all airline pilots, business executives, streetcar conductors, or bronco busters to be male.

Avoid using occupational terms with feminine suffixes: *actor/actress, author/authoress, poet/poetess.* Such feminine forms have become obsolete, and the formerly male form has become neutral: *author, poet, actor,* and *executor.* Others, such as *waitress,* are changing to more inclusive terms: *server* or *wait-staff,* for example. Similarly, avoid occupational terms that end in *–man,* which imply that everyone who holds a particular job is male.

CHECKLIST OF OCCUPATIONAL LABELS

SEXIST	NEUTRAL
statesman	diplomat
mailman	letter carrier, mail carrier
policeman	police officer
fireman	firefighter
businessman	executive, businessperson
salesman	sales representative
chairman	chairperson, chair

51 d Eliminating stereotypes

As you edit, ask these four questions:

1. Have I relied on stereotypes rather than on evidence to make my point? Are all African Americans "good dancers"?

2. Do my generalizations follow logically from factual evidence? If "they're all crazy," do you mean *all* of them? Literally *crazy*?

3. Do my generalizations about a group improperly label individuals: Is it true that "students these days can't write"? (You know the truth of this one.)

4. Have I used euphemism to mask a stereotype? Is a woman "a wonderful asset to her husband" or something more in her own right?

PART ten

Editing for Grammar

The term **grammar** refers to patterns of the customary use of language, patterns that help listeners and readers understand. The "rules" of grammar are, at heart, descriptions of those patterns, and writers follow them not only to be "correct" but to lessen the chance of being misunderstood.

52 | *Sentence Fragments*

An English sentence expresses a complete idea; a sentence fragment does not. A group of words punctuated as a sentence that lacks a subject or a verb is a fragment. Another kind of fragment begins with a word such as *if, when, although,* or *because,* which makes it unable to stand alone as a sentence. Although fragments appear in everyday speech, in academic writing they are among the errors that make instructors most uncomfortable.

52 a Fragments lacking verbs or subjects

A group of words punctuated as a sentence that lacks a subject or a verb is a fragment.

> A fleet of colorful fishing boats $\overset{\text{was}}{\underset{\wedge}{\text{rocking}}}$ at anchor in the bay.

> *The -ing form of a verb cannot serve as the main verb of a sentence without an auxiliary (see 54d).*

> The bale of shingles started to slip. $\overset{\text{It slid}}{\underset{\wedge}{\text{Slid}}}$ right off the roof.

> **Slid right off the roof** *has no subject.*

52 b Dependent clause fragments

A dependent clause has a subject and a verb but begins with a word such as *after, although, since, because, when, where,* or *whether,* so that it makes no sense standing alone.

> None of us understood the result $\overset{\text{, even}}{\underset{\wedge}{\text{Even}}}$ though the instructor explained it.

52 c Intentional fragments

Writers occasionally use fragments to reproduce the sound of spoken language or create dramatic emphasis in fiction, personal essays, and wherever dialogue is reproduced.

I knew that I was no legitimate resident in any world of ideas. I knew I couldn't think. All I knew then was what I couldn't do. All I knew then was what I wasn't, and it took me some years to discover what I was.

Which was a writer.

By which I mean not a "good" writer or a "bad" writer, but simply a writer, a person whose most absorbed and passionate hours are spent arranging words on pieces of paper.

Joan Didion, "Why I Write" [italics added]

If you want to use a fragment for emphasis, think about its effect, and make sure that it seems intentional. When your point warrants disrupting readers' expectations, consider using a fragment. If it works.

53 | Run-On Sentences and Comma Splices

Two sentences can be joined into one. There are several ways to do so correctly.

Two sentences can be joined into one, and there are several ways to do so correctly.

Two sentences can be joined into one; there are several ways to do so correctly.

There are also two common ways of doing it wrong. A **run-on sentence** provides no hint that one independent clause is ending and another beginning:

Everyone was asked to give an opinion on the plan , but Mr. Smith was out of town.

The teachers thought the plan might not work , and the students were sure it wouldn't.

A **comma splice** uses only a comma to mark the joining.

Professional athletes can earn huge salaries ; some are paid millions of dollars a year.

53 a Comma and coordinating conjunction

When a coordinating conjunction (*and, but, or, nor, for, yet, so*) joins independent clauses, it must be preceded by a comma.

> Maya Angelou has worked as an actor and as
>
> a director ,but her greatest success came as an
>
> autobiographer and poet.
>
> *The coordinating conjunction and the comma are both necessary.*

53 b Semicolon

Use a semicolon to join two independent clauses whose ideas are closely related. If the relationship between the two clauses is not clear, make them separate sentences, or use a coordinating conjunction.

> For years the Federal Communications Commission
>
> advocated competitive auctions for broadcast
>
> licenses ;so far Congress has refused.

Use a semicolon between independent clauses linked with a conjunctive adverb such as *however* or *therefore* or a transitional phrase like *in fact* or *for example*.

> The mayor presented her budget plans; <u>however</u>, the council had its own ideas.

Use a colon to join two independent clauses when the second clause explains, elaborates, or illustrates the first.

> It was not a perfect season: we lost one game.

53 c Separate sentences

When one clause is much longer, or different in structure, rewrite the two independent clauses as separate sentences.

> My last year of high school was an eventful one ~~and~~ . Everything
>
> ~~everything~~ seemed to be happening all at once.

53 d   Using subordination

Emphasize the main idea in your sentences, and place the less important idea in a dependent clause. Choose the subordinating conjunction (*after, as, because, before, if, than, that, when,* etc.) that best describes the relationship you want to establish between the two.

> Because the
> ~~The~~ rain had frozen as it hit the ground, the streets
> ^
> were slippery.

---

54   Using Verbs Correctly

Verbs drive sentences the way engines power cars. Select correct verb forms that convey the meaning you intend.

TERMS USED TO DESCRIBE VERBS

Person indicates who performs an action: *I read, you read, he reads.*

Number indicates how many people (or things) perform the action: *she thinks, they think*

Tense indiates the time of the action: *I learn, I learned, I will learn.*

Mood expresses the speaker's attitude toward the action: *He* is *quiet.* Be *quiet! I would be happier if he* were *quiet.*

54 a   Standard verb forms

Except for the verb *be,* all English verbs have five forms.

To express **present action:**

Base form: I *act.*

-s form (he, she, it): He *acts.*

To express **past action:**

Past tense (-d, -ed + base form): I *acted.*

Past participle (form of *be* or *have* + past participle): I *have acted.*

Present participle (-*ing* + base form) expresses continuing action: (in present and past tense): I am *acting.* I was *acting.* (See 54d.)

Verbs that follow these patterns are called *regular;* those that form the past tense and past participle in other ways are called *irregular* (see 54b).

Using -*s* and -*ed* Forms

Except for the verbs *be* and *have,* -*s* or -*es* is the ending for third person singular verbs in the **present tense.**

The baby *sleeps.*

Everyone at the party *dances.*

Though nonstandard usage is sometimes used (for example, to reproduce dialects), academic writing requires standard verb usage.

He ~~don't~~ need to study.

doesn't

The **past tense** of all regular verbs is created by adding -*d* or -*ed* to the base form: *dance, danced.*

54 b Irregular verb forms

Verbs that do not follow the pattern of adding -*d* or -*ed* to form the past tense and past participle are called **irregular.** Some irregular verbs (*bet, bid, burst, cost, cut, hit, hurt, let, quit, rid, set*) do not change in any form:

I *hit* the ball now, but I *hit* it better yesterday. In the past, I *have hit* it even better. Some others (*ring, sing, spring, drink, stink*) have a pattern of vowel changes:

I *ring* the bell today, I *rang* it yesterday as I have *rung* it every morning. But see *bring, cling, sting* and *swing* in the list of irregular verbs.

Be is the most irregular verb.

Base form	be
Present	am, are, is [-s form]
Past	was, were
Present participle	being
Past participle	been

Common Irregular Verbs

BASE FORM	PAST TENSE	PAST PARTICIPLE
arise	arose	arisen
awake	awoke, awakened	awakened, awoken
be	was, were	been
bear	bore	born
beat	beat	beaten, beat
become	became	become
begin	began	begun
bend	bent	bent
bite	bit	bitten
blow	blew	blown
break	broke	broken
bring	brought	brought
build	built	built
buy	bought	bought
catch	caught	caught
choose	chose	chosen
come	came	come
creep	crept	crept
dig	dug	dug
dive	dived, dove	dived
do	did	done
draw	drew	drawn
drive	drove	driven
eat	ate	eaten
fall	fell	fallen
feed	fed	fed
feel	felt	felt
fight	fought	fought
find	found	found
fly	flew	flown
forbid	forbade	forbidden
forget	forgot	forgotten
freeze	froze	frozen
get	got	gotten, got
give	gave	given
go	went	gone
grow	grew	grown
hang (suspend)	hung	hung
hang (execute)	hanged	hanged
have	had	had

hear	heard	heard
hide	hid	hidden
hold	held	held
keep	kept	kept
know	knew	known
lay (put)	laid	laid
lead	led	led
leap	leapt, leaped	leapt, leaped
leave	left	left
lend	lent	lent
lie (recline)	lay	lain
light	lit, lighted	lit, lighted
lose	lost	lost
make	made	made
mean	meant	meant
meet	met	met
pay	paid	paid
prove	proved	proved, proven
read	read (pronounced red)	read (pronounced red)
ride	rode	ridden
ring	rang	rung
rise	rose	risen
run	ran	run
say	said	said
see	saw	seen
seek	sought	sought
send	sent	sent
shake	shook	shaken
shoot	shot	shot
show	showed	shown, showed
shrink	shrank	shrunk
sit	sat	sat
sleep	slept	slept
speak	spoke	spoken
spin	spun	spun
spit	spit, spat	spit, spat
stand	stood	stood
steal	stole	stolen
stick	stuck	stuck
sting	stung	stung
strike	struck	struck, stricken
swear	swore	sworn
swim	swam	swum
swing	swung	swung

(continued)

take	took	taken
teach	taught	taught
tear	tore	torn
tell	told	told
think	thought	thought
throw	threw	thrown
wear	wore	worn
win	won	won
write	wrote	written

54 c   *Sit* and *set, lie* and *lay*

Because these words sound similar and are related in meaning, they are often confused. They are really very different.

Set and *lay* mean "to place" and need an object to complete their meaning (what are they placing?). They are called **transitive verbs** and are said to "take a direct object."

dir. object   dir. object

I *set* the <u>table</u> each morning before I *lay* the <u>mail</u> on the desk.

Sit ("to be seated") and *lie* ("to recline") need no object to complete their meaning, and are called **intransitive verbs.**

I will *sit* outside for a while, but soon I'll want to *lie* down.

This particular verb gets particularly confusing since the past tense of *lie* is *lay!* To use these correctly, first establish your meaning (Are you setting or laying something? Or are you just enjoying yourself sitting and lying down?), and refer to this chart. Be sure to use the correct form of each of these troublesome verbs.

The books were ~~laying~~ lying on the table.

She asked me to come in and ~~set~~ sit with her a while.

54 d   Auxiliary verbs

In certain situations, an **auxiliary** or **helping verb,** commonly a form of *be, have,* or *do,* is needed to form the main verb of a sentence.

verb phrase (main verb)

auxiliary   present participle

Tyler   *is*   *working.*

Auxiliary verbs do various jobs:

The student council *is considering* what to do about it.

(present progressive tense)

They *do want* to go to the conference.

(emphasis)

Has he *received* the blueprints?

(question)

He *does* not *intend* to leave without them.

(negative statement)

The blueprints *were delivered* on Friday.

(passive voice)

Have, do, and *be* change form to indicate tense

I *have mended* a jacket that *had been* torn.

Modal Auxiliaries

Can, could, may, might, must, shall, should, will, and *would* are used with a main verb to express condition, intent, permission, possibility, obligation, or desire (and certain tenses, see 54e). These **modal auxiliaries** cannot stand alone as a main verb; they always appear with the base form of the verb unless the context creates necessary meaning. They do not change form.

Staying in touch with friends *can become* difficult as we grow old.

Can she *dance?* Yes, she *can.*

*(*dance *is understood here)*

Using Auxiliary Verbs Correctly

Standard English requires auxiliary verbs *be* or *have* with present participles and past participles.

is

Gina running for student council.

has

She spoken to everyone about it.

A form of *be—is, are, was, were*—with the past participle is needed to create the passive voice.

Each student *is given* a book upon graduation.

Transitive and Intransitive Verbs

Some verbs require a direct object, a word or words that indicate who or what received the action of the verb.

direct object
They documented *their results.*

A verb that has a direct object is a **transitive** verb. A verb that does not have a direct object is an **intransitive** verb. Many verbs may be either transitive or intransitive, depending on the context.

TRANSITIVE
Joey grew tomatoes last summer.

INTRANSITIVE
The tomatoes grew rapidly.

Linking Verbs

Linking verbs include *be, become, seem,* and verbs describing sensations—*appear, look, feel, taste, smell.* They link the subject of a sentence to a **subject complement,** an element that renames or describes the subject. A linking verb, like an equal sign, links two equivalent terms.

Sue is helpful.   Sue = helpful
They felt tired.   They = tired
Jake is the captain. Jake = captain

54 e   Verb tense

The **tense** of a verb indicates the time of its action. **Present** tense describes something occurring at the time of speaking.

He *looks* happy today. He usually *looks* pretty content.

The present also is used to state general facts or truths and in writing about literature.

In *The Tempest*, the wizard Prospero *seems* to control the heavens.

The **past** tense describes actions completed in the past.

He *looked* a little depressed yesterday.

The **future** tense describes actions that will occur in the future.

> He *will arrive* tomorrow.

The three **perfect tenses** indicate action completed by a specific time. Using forms of *have* + the past participle, they place that completion in the present, past, or future. **Present perfect** describes action completed in the past.

> She *has worked* hard.

It also can imply an action continuing into the present

> She *has worked* hard all week.

Past perfect describes action completed before another past action occurred.

> She *had looked* for the file several times before she found it.

Future perfect describes an action that will be completed at some specific time in the future.

> Once she goes through the last drawer, she *will have looked* everywhere.

The three **progressive tenses** describe *continuing action*. **Present progressive** describes ongoing action in the present.

> She *is anticipating* the holidays.

Past progressive describes continuous action in the past with no specified end.

> Before her father's illness, she *was anticipating* the holidays.

Future progressive demonstrates continuous or ongoing action in the future that often depends on some other action or circumstance.

> Once her father is better, she *will be anticipating* the holidays again.

The three **perfect progressive** tenses describe action continuing up to a point in the present, past, or future. **Present perfect progressive** describes action that began in the past and continues.

> He *has been looking* for a job since August.

Past perfect progressive describes ongoing action completed in the past.

> Before he found work, he *had been looking* for a job since August.

Future perfect progressive describes continuing action that will be completed at some future time.

> By August, he *will have been looking* for a job for six months.

54 f   Sequence of tenses

Many combinations of verb tenses are possible in the same sentence. The sequence of tenses must describe events accurately and make sense.

> present   future
> I <u>think</u> that you <u>will enjoy</u> this movie.
> *(I am thinking this before you go to the movie.)*

> present   present
> I <u>know</u> that you <u>like</u> foreign films.
> *(I am knowing this at the same time you are liking foreign films.)*

> present   past
> I <u>believe</u> that you <u>misunderstood</u> me.
> *(I believe this after you misunderstood me.)*

54 g   Mood

English has three different moods:

1. **Indicative** mood states facts, opinions, and questions.

   He believes *the theory is valid.*

2. **Imperative** mood is used for commands.

   Knead *the dough until it forms a ball.*

3. **Subjunctive** mood expresses wishes, requirements, or conditions contrary to fact.

   If he were *more dedicated, he would practice more often.*

54 h Voice

The voice of a verb tells you if the subject is the actor **(active voice)** or the receiver of the action **(passive voice).** The active voice is considered simpler, more direct, and thus more quickly understood by the reader.

She *read* the book. *(active voice)*

The book *was read* by her. *(passive voice)*

55 Subject–Verb Agreement

Verbs must agree with their subjects in number (one or more than one?) and person (Who is acting? I? You? He, she, or it? They?). Matters of agreement often come down to the addition of the letter *–s* as in third person singular:

	SINGULAR	PLURAL
1st person:	I think	We think
2nd person:	You think	You think
3rd person:	He/she/it/thinks	They think

This works for many verbs in common usage. However, the verb *be* has very different forms in the past and present tenses:

PRESENT TENSE		PAST TENSE	
SINGULAR	PLURAL	SINGULAR	PLURAL
I am	we are	I was	we were
you are	you are	you were	you were
he/she/it is	they are	he/she/it was	they were

55 a Interruptions between subject and verb

Words placed between the subject and verb sometimes confuse the issue. Mentally eliminate the interrupting words and test for the proper match.

The bowl of apples ~~are~~ *is* very tempting.

(Translate sentence to The bowl . . . is very tempting. Singular subject, bowl, takes singular verb, is.)

Mr. Johnson, along with his children, ~~were~~ waiting
outside.

*(Translate sentence to Mr. Johnson . . . was waiting outside.
Singular subject, Mr. Johnson, takes singular verb, was.)*

55 b   Subjects linked by *and*

Two or more subjects linked by *and* (compound subjects)
are almost always plural:

Peter and Patrick *play* on the lacrosse team.

Exception: When the two joined words comprise a single entity, it requires a singular verb:

Red beans and rice *is* my favorite dish.

55 c   Subjects joined by *or* or *nor*

Make verb agree with the subject closer to it.

Neither the researchers nor the professor *accepts*
the results.

Singular professor is closer to verb; use singular verb.

Neither the professor nor the researchers *accept* the
results.

Plural researchers is closer to verb; use plural verb.

55 d   Collective nouns

Words that refer to groups of people, animals, or things
(*couple, flock, crowd, herd, committee*) are called **collective
nouns.** Such words can take either singular or plural verbs,
depending if you consider the group as a single unit or a
composite of individuals.

The jury *has* reached a verdict.

The group, jury, is acting as one and takes a singular verb.

The couple *disagree.*

*The individuals of the couple are acting separately. Use a
plural verb.*

Media, data, curricula, criteria, and *phenomena* look
like singular words, but, in fact, they are the plurals (from

Greek and Latin sources) of *medium, datum, criterion,* and *phenomenon.* These words should take *plural* verbs:

> The media ~~has~~ *have* continued to focus on crime even as
>
> data ~~shows~~ *show* that cities are becoming safer.

55 e Indefinite pronouns

Indefinite pronouns do not refer to *specific* persons or things. *Anybody, anyone, anything, each, either, everybody, everyone, everything, neither, no one, one, somebody, someone,* and *something* are considered singular and take singular verbs.

> Someone *has* been sleeping in my bed.
>
> Everybody *wears* a heavy coat in this weather.

All, any, and *some* can be singular or plural.

> All *are* required to take the exam.
>
> All I have *is* a rough idea.

None, which means "not one," takes a singular verb:

> The birds all escaped, and none *was* recaptured.

55 f *Who, which,* and *that*

To match the verb to your pronoun, consider the word to which it refers.

> Barb and Robin, who want to join the project, have applied.

Who refers to plural *Barb and Robin,* and therefore takes a plural verb.

> A box of nails *is* about three pounds.
>
> In this sentence, *is* refers to singular *box.*

55 g Nouns ending in *-s*

Statistics, politics, economics, athletics, measles, news, acoustics, and *aesthetics* appear to be plural nouns, but they take singular verbs.

Economics *is* sometimes called "the dismal science."

Exception: When these nouns refer to specific instances or characteristics, they are considered plural.

The economics of the project *make* no sense.

55 h   Titles used as words

Titles involving more than one word are considered singular and take a singular verb.

"Shake, Rattle, and Roll" *was* recorded by Bill Haley and the Comets.

General Motors *is* an important employer in Michigan.

56 | Pronouns

A pronoun is a stand-in for a noun: *she, it, them, me,* and so on. Problems with pronouns usually arise in these three areas:

Reference   Is it clear to whom the pronoun refers?
Agreement   Does it "agree with," or match, the noun to which it refers in gender and number?
Case   When do you use *I* or *me? Who* or *whom?*

56 a   Reference

The word to which a pronoun refers is called its *antecedent.* Problems occur when an antecedent is unclear.

UNCLEAR
Marco met Roger as he arrived at the gym.
(Who arrived?)

SPECIFIC
As Marco arrived at the gym, he met Roger.

or

Marco met Roger as Roger arrived at the gym.

If there is no appropriate word to serve as an antecedent, you might have to provide one.

Interviews with several television news people

made ~~it~~ seem like a fascinating career.
     reporting (inserted)

Without an explicit antecedent, the reader doesn't know what seems fascinating.

Vague Reference with *this, that,* and *which*

Make sure it's clear what *this, that,* or *which* refers to.

No one has suggested taxing health care. This ~~tax~~ is unlikely.
    tax (inserted)

Without the added word, it's unclear whether the suggestion or the tax is unlikely.

Vague Reference with *it, they,* or *you*

In casual speech, vague antecedents are common, but academic writing requires explicit reference.

~~It said on~~ the news this morning ~~that~~ the game was canceled.
    According to , (inserted)

~~They don't~~ let anyone in without a shirt or shoes.
    The club doesn't (inserted)

56 b   Agreement

Personal pronouns should agree with their antecedents in number, person, and gender.

Mrs. Ramos held the door for *her* daughter.

Singular, feminine her *refers to Mrs. Ramos.*

The Shaws were on *their* way to the antique show.

Plural pronoun their *refers to more than one Shaw.*

In Gender

Because *anyone, someone,* and *everyone* can refer to either gender, take care in choosing pronouns that refer to them. Here are two common problems.

If *anyone* needs to miss class, *he* must contact the instructor.

The masculine he *and the gender-neutral* anyone *do not agree.*

If *anyone* needs to miss class, *they* must contact the instructor.

The plural they *does not agree with the singular* anyone.

To address these problems, (1) use *he or she* or *his or her*, (2) use *students* in place of *anyone*, or (3) eliminate personal pronouns: *Students who miss class must contact the instructor.*

With Antecedents Joined by *and*

Pronouns referring to a compound antecedent should be plural.

The *book and the folders* are in *their* places on the shelf.

With Antecedents Joined by *or* and *nor*

Make your pronoun agree with the antecedent closer to it.

Either the equipment failures or the bad *weather* will take *its* toll.

Singular its *refers to the closer antecedent,* weather.

With Collective Nouns

Use a plural pronoun to refer to collective nouns (e.g., *couple, flock, crowd*) that are seen as a single unit.

The flock rose suddenly from the pond and took up
~~their~~ its usual formation.

With Indefinite Pronouns

Anyone, everyone, someone, anybody, everybody, somebody, anything, everything, something, either, neither, each, nothing, much, one, none, and *no one* are always singular.

Neither of these books has ~~their~~ its original cover.

Few, many, both, and *several* are always plural and therefore require a plural pronoun.

Few of the students have completed *their* work.

The indefinite pronouns *some, any, all, more,* and *most* can be singular or plural depending on their context.

Among the students, *some* said *they* were conservative.

Some of the grain has spoiled; *it* must have gotten wet.

56 c   Case

Pronouns perform various roles in sentences, just as nouns do. These different roles are called *cases*. Use *subjective case* of pronoun for a subject, the person or thing that performs action in the sentence: <u>She</u> *plays piano*. Use objective case when a pronoun receives the action: *Bob congratulated <u>her</u>*. Use possessive case to show ownership. <u>My</u> *cousin lives in the city. The book you are reading is <u>hers</u>*.

SUBJECTIVE	OBJECTIVE	POSSESSIVE	
		BEFORE A NOUN	STANDING ALONE
I	me	my	mine
you	you	your	yours
he/she/it	him/her/it	his/her/its	his/hers/its
we	us	our	ours
you	you	your	yours
they	them	their	theirs

Compound Subjects

Choosing the correct pronoun can be tricky when two subjects are joined by *and*. Test the sentence with only the pronoun to determine the correct pronoun.

> I
> Todd and ~~me~~ pruned the tall white pine.
> ^
> **When you test the sentence as Me pruned the tall white pine, the correct choice is clear.**

Complements

Complements rename subjects, following linking verbs: *The winner was my dad. Winner* and *dad* are the same people, linked by verb *was*. When there is a compound complement, use subjective case.

> I.
> The winners were Gina and ~~me.~~
> ^

Compound Objects

Objects joined by *and, or,* or *nor* should be in the objective case.

> Just between you and ~~I~~, it's a fake.
> _{me}
>
> I spoke with Nancy and ~~they~~ about the competition.
> _{them}

Appositives

Appositives, which rename nouns or pronouns, must have the same case as the words they rename.

> It was the victors, Paul and *he*, who wanted to leave.
>
> *Appositive* Paul and he *is in the subjective case.*
>
> They asked the teachers, Barbara and *me*, to help out.
>
> *Appositive* Barbara and me *is in the objective case.*

We or *us* before a Noun

To choose the correct case for a pronoun preceding a noun, omit the noun and test.

> ~~Us~~ hikers were worried about the weather.
> ^{We}
>
> They told ~~we~~ hikers not to worry.
> _{us}

With Verbals

Verbals are forms derived from verbs. When a pronoun is the object of a verbal, use the objective case.

> **PARTICIPLE** (-ing form)
> *I saw Robert greeting <u>him</u>.*
>
> **GERUND** (-ing form used as a noun)
> *Seeing <u>her</u> made the holiday complete.*
>
> **INFINITIVE** (base verb preceded by *to*)
> *Everyone seems to know <u>him</u>.*

Use possessive case when a pronoun precedes a gerund (a verbal used as a noun).

> ~~Me~~ leaving made them all sad.
> ^{My}

Use objective case for pronouns before infinitives.

>They want *her* to help.

After *than* or *as*

To choose case following *than* or *as,* mentally supply the missing words:

>She likes her dog better than (me? I?)

Construct test sentences that include the possible missing words:

>She likes her dog better than I (like her dog).

>She likes her dog better than (she likes) me.

56 d   *Who* or *whom*

The distinction between *who* and *whom* has all but disappeared from everyday speech, but in writing use *who* for subjects and *whom* for objects.

In Questions

To choose *who* or *whom* in a question, turn the question into a statement by substituting *he* or *him.* If *he* fits, use *who.* If *him* fits, use *whom.*

>*Who/whom* had the authority to enter the building at night?

>He *had the authority, so use* who.

>To *who/whom* are you speaking?

>*You are speaking to* him, *so use* whom.

In Dependent Clauses

In choosing *who* or *whom* in a dependent clause, determine the word's function within the clause.

>   *whom*
>That woman, ~~who~~ I met last week, won the Nobel
>   ^
>prize for chemistry.

>Whom *is the object of* met, *even though it renames the subject of the main clause,* woman.

>   *whoever*
>She tells that same story to ~~whomever~~ will listen.
>   ^

>Whoever *is the subject of* will listen. *Choose according to the role of* who/whom *in the clause it introduces.*

57 Using Adjectives and Adverbs

Adjectives modify (describe, identify, or limit) nouns or pronouns.

> Hector is *a fine* father who has *gentle* hands and
> *abundant* patience with *crying* babies.

> He is loving, careful, and dependable.

Adjectives usually come before nouns, but they can also come after a linking verb such as *be, become, appear, grow, seem, remind,* and *approve: The ghost of Hamlet's father seems* vengeful.

Appear, look, smell, taste, and *sound* can also function as action verbs. If you are describing an action, use an adverb: *The ghost of Hamlet's father appears* suddenly.

Adverbs modify verbs, adjectives, other adverbs, and sometimes whole clauses.

> He *often* takes care of the baby at *truly* late hours
> and *nearly always* quiets her *quickly.*

Adverbs tell *when, where, how, why,* and *under what conditions* something happens. An adverb that modifies an adjective often intensifies (*deeply sorry*) or limits it (*barely awake*).

Adjectives are often formed by adding endings such as *-able, -ful,* and *-ish* to nouns and verbs: *acceptable, beautiful, foolish.* Adverbs are sometimes formed by adding *ly* to an adjective: *nearly, amazingly, brilliantly.* However, an *-ly* suffix does not always mean that a word is an adverb. A number of adjectives end in *-ly: brotherly, friendly, lovely.* And many adverbs do not end in *-ly: always, here.*

57 a   Common confusions

In casual speech, adjectives are sometimes used instead of adverbs to modify verbs: *It fit real well* instead of *It fit really well.* Be sure to use the correct forms of the following pairs.

Bad and *badly*

In academic writing, use *bad* only as an adjective with a linking verb and *badly* as an adverb with other verbs.

She looked as though she felt ~~badly~~ *bad*.

They were playing so ~~bad~~ *badly* that I left at halftime.

Good and *well*

Good is always an adjective; *well* can be either an adjective meaning "healthy" or an adverb meaning "skillfully."

She sings ~~good~~ *well* enough to get the lead.

The hat looked ~~well~~ *good* on my mother.

Less and *fewer*

Less and *fewer* are both adjectives, but they function in different ways. *Less* describes something considered as a whole unit: *less hope, less money*. *Fewer* describes quantities that can be counted: *fewer hopes, fewer dollars*.

The house would lose *less* heat if ~~less~~ *fewer* windows were open.

57 b   Comparatives and superlatives

The **positive** form of an adjective or adverb describes a particular property (*smart, funny*). The **comparative** makes a comparison between **two** people or things (*smarter, funnier, more abundant*). The **superlative** form makes a comparison among **three or more** (*smartest, funniest, most abundant*).

Adjectives of two or more syllables generally use *more* and *most* in their comparative and superlative forms. Negative comparisons are formed using *less* and *least*.

POSITIVE	COMPARATIVE	SUPERLATIVE
big	bigger	biggest
fast	faster	fastest
good	better	best
careful	more careful	most careful
hopeful	less hopeful	least hopeful

Choosing comparative or superlative can let readers know what you're comparing.

Of the brothers, Joe was the *stronger* athlete. (There are two brothers.)

Of the brothers, Joe was the *strongest* athlete. (There are at least three brothers.)

When forming comparatives, use *-er* or *more,* not both. In superlatives, use either *-est* or *most,* not both.

After eating, he felt ~~more~~ better.

57 c   Double negatives

In English, one negative modifier (*no, not, never*) changes the meaning of a sentence. Two negatives cancel each other: *I did<u>n't</u> have <u>no</u> money* literally means *I did have some money.* Avoid double negatives.

58   Modifier Placement

In English, word order affects meaning. *The man ate the fish* is not the same as *The fish ate the man.*

58 a   Misplaced modifiers

Modifiers should point clearly to the words they modify. As a rule, related words should be kept together. A misplaced modifier can suggest a meaning other than the one the writer intended: *We wanted our ordeal to end desperately.*

Unless the writer wanted things to turn out badly, the modifier is misplaced. Put the modifier (*desperately*) as close as possible to the word it modifies (*wanted*) to clarify: *We desperately wanted our ordeal to end.*

Limiting Modifiers

Put limiting modifiers, such as *almost, even, hardly, just, merely, nearly, only, scarcely,* or *simply,* directly before the words they modify:

only
We want what is ~~only~~ ours.
^

58 b   Dangling modifiers

A modifier is said to be "dangling" when the subject it is supposed to modify is missing. Look out for dangling modifiers at the beginning of sentences.

> Running through the rain, our clothes got soaked.

This sentence suggest that *our clothes* were running through the rain. The actor of the sentence—*we*—is missing. To correct a dangling modifier place the subject directly after the modifier, and supply a new verb if necessary.

> Running through the rain, our clothes ~~got~~ soaked.
>   we got ^

58 c   Split infinitives

An infinitive consists of *to* plus a verb: *to fly, to grow, to achieve.* When a modifier comes between its two parts, an infinitive is "split": *to barely try.* Many writers and teachers find split infinitives annoying, so look for alternatives.

> She needed to ~~carefully~~ consider the decision.
>   carefully. ^

59   English as a Second Language (ESL)

This chapter is designed to offer tips on some issues that arise for students who are learning English as a second language.

59 a   Articles *a, an, the*

The articles *the, a,* and *an* are used to introduce nouns. Sometimes they come directly in front of the noun; other times they come before a modifier.

> the dog, the large dog; a car, a red car; an apple, an edible apple

When to Use *a* (or *an*)

Use *a* or *an* with singular words that name persons, places, or things that can be counted (count nouns): *a bird, two birds; a chair, two chairs*. Use *a* or *an* when the item in question has not yet been specified.

> She bought *a car* by reading *an advertisement* in the paper.

A is used before a consonant sound: *a bowl, a happy person. An* is used before a vowel sound: *an insect, an honest person*.

When Not to Use *a* (or *an*)

A and *an* are not used for nouns that refer to abstractions or things that cannot be counted (noncount words): *water, oil, sand, money*.

> The boys brought ~~a~~ sand from the beach.

Express a specific amount in terms of a measurement: *a stick of butter, a gallon of water*.

COMMON NONCOUNT NOUNS

Food and drink: *bacon, fish, milk, tea*

Nonfood substances: *air, coal, dirt, paper*

Areas of study: *art, biology, economics, history*

Ideas and emotions: *anger, beauty, health, love*

Other: *clothing, equipment, furniture, homework, jewelry*

When to Use *the*

Use the definite article *the* with count nouns in the following cases.

1. The noun has already been mentioned.

   There is *a* problem *(not previously specified)* with this approach. *The* problem *(the one just identified)* is *a* difficult one.

2. The noun is made specific by modifiers.

   The man *in the blue suit* is the mayor.

   The phrase in the blue suit *identifies the specific man.*

3. The context makes the noun specific.

Please open *the* window.

Both the speaker and the listener know which window is meant.

When Not to Use *the*

Do not use *the* with plural nouns or with noncount nouns that mean "all" or "in general."

Milk
~~The milk~~ is an important source of calcium.

Do not use *the* with singular proper nouns such as names of people (*Abraham Lincoln*); names of streets, parks, cities, and states (*Union Street, Glacier National Park, Boston, Maine*); names of continents and most countries (*Asia, Peru*); and names of bays and single lakes, mountains, and islands (*Penobscott Bay, Lake Superior, Mount Washington, Bermuda*).

Exceptions include regions, deserts, and peninsulas (*the West Coast, the Sahara Desert, the Yucatan Peninsula*) and the names of oceans, seas, gulfs, canals, and rivers (*the Atlantic, the Black Sea, the Gulf of Mexico, the Panama Canal, the Ohio River*).

But use *the* with plural proper nouns: *the United States, the Great Lakes, the Green Mountains, the Bahamas*.

59 b Two-word verbs

Some verbs join a second word—such as *on, by, up, over,* or *through*—to create a new meaning. Here are some examples of such two-word verbs:

VERB	PARTICLE	MEANING
call	off	cancel
call	out	summon
find	out	discover, learn
get	through	finish
make	up	invent, create
put	off	postpone
see	through	finish; not be deceived by
see	off	bid farewell
see	to	pay attention to

Here are some guidelines for using two-word verbs:

- If the verb has no direct object, put the particle directly after the verb.

    The photocopy machine *breaks down* often.

    or

    The photocopy machine often *breaks down*.

    Some other two-word verbs in this group are *come back, come over, play around, lie down, roll over,* and *turn back* (retreat).

- Two-word verbs with direct objects follow one of these four patterns:

    1. Those that cannot be separated

    Please *go over* this report carefully.

    Watch your step as you *step off* the platform.

    Other verbs that follow this pattern include *come across, get on, get off, get over, get through* (finish), *look into,* and *see through* (not be deceived by).

    2. Those that must be separated by the direct object

    I tried to *get* the idea *across* to him.

    I had to insist that he *do* it *over*.

    Only a few two-part verbs follow this pattern, including *get across* (communicate) and *see through* (finish).

    3. Those that need not be separated by a noun object but must be separated if a pronoun is the object

    You can write:

    The governor *called out* the National Guard to help in the flood.

    or

    The governor *called* the National Guard *out* to help in the flood.

    However, if the direct object is a pronoun, the verb parts must be separated.

    The light was shining in my eyes, so I asked her to *turn* it *off*.

    Many two-word verbs follow this pattern: *fill out, find out, give up, look over, leave out, make*

up, put down, put on, put away, turn off, turn on,
and *turn back* (reverse).

4. Those that separate if a pronoun is the object

You can write:

I *picked up* the mail.

or

I *picked* it *up.* (but not *I picked up it.*)

Verbs that follow this pattern include many
that use *up, down, in,* or *out.*

If you are not sure how to use a two-word verb, consult an ESL dictionary or a native speaker.

59 c Prepositions

Prepositional phrases can indicate time, location, place, or
direction. Here is a list of common prepositions that begin
such phrases.

Time

at noon, *at* night, *at* breakfast time

With dates: *in* 1999, *in* the twenty-first century, *in*
the afternoon, *on* Monday, *on* October 3

In a limited time: *by* next Thursday, *by* Thanksgiving

In a particular time period: *during* the day

until (any time before and up to a specified point):
until today, *until* 8:00, *until* now

Place

at the table, *at* home, *at* school, *at* the corner, *at* the
subway station

in a room, *in* Canada, *in* the world, *in* class, *in* the car

on the desk, *on* the radio, *on* the wall, *on* a plane

Direction

arrive *from* Australia, *from* your house, *from* another
planet

go *to* a place: *to* Canada, *to* school, *to* church

fall *off* something: *off* a bike, *off* the roof

travel *around* an area: *around* Europe, *around* town

snowboard *down* something: *down* the hill

59 d Order of adjectives

The order of adjectives preceding nouns is somewhat flexible, but some kinds of adjectives typically occur before others. For example, an adjective describing size occurs before one describing color: *the large white house* rather than *the white large house.*

The following list shows the typical order of adjectives before nouns.

1 Determiner: *a, the, her, Bob's, that, these*

2 Order, number: *first, next, one, two, few, several*

3 Evaluation: *good, pretty, happy, interesting*

4 Appearance—size: *big, small, minuscule*

5 Appearance—shape: *oblong, squarish, round*

6 Appearance—condition: *broken, shiny*

7 Appearance—age: *old, young, new*

8 Appearance—color: *blue, green, magenta*

9 Material: *wooden, cotton*

10 Noun used as adjective: *garden* hose

```
              1     2     6     7     10
```
One never forgets that first shiny new sports car.
```
1  2     4     5     9      10
```
A few large square wooden crab pots were stacked on the floor.

PART eleven

Editing Punctuation

The more carefully you punctuate, the more easily readers will understand you. Commas, semicolons, dashes, parentheses, and other punctuation marks help indicate the structure of your sentences. Misusing any of these signals can cause misunderstanding or loss of meaning.

60   *End Punctuation*

Your choice of end punctuation helps to distinguish among statements, exclamations, and questions.

60 a   Periods

Use a period at the end of a statement, a mild command, or a polite request.

> The breeze is very chilly. Please close the door.

Use a period, not a question mark, after an indirect question (a question that is reported but not asked directly).

> I wonder who made that decision.

Use a single period when an abbreviation containing a period falls at the end of a sentence.

> Her flight leaves at 6:15 A.M. His departs at 7:00.

Use a period after abbreviations that end in lowercase letters.

> Mr. Mrs. Ms. Dr. Rev. Msgr. Gov. Sen. in.
> ft. etc. e.g. i.e. vs. Tue. Jan. St. Ave. p.
> para. fig. vol.

Exceptions: mph, rpm

Do not use periods in other abbreviations unless they stand for personal names.

> US UK BC BCE AD BA PhD MD *but*
> W.E.B. DuBois

Do not use periods with acronyms (initials pronounced as words) or with the abbreviated names of government agencies, corporations, and other entities.

> NASA NATO AIDS CNN SAT FBI CIA EPA
> IRS IRA NCAA

60 b   Question marks

Use question marks at the end of direct questions. (Direct questions are usually signaled either by *what, where,* or *why,* or by inverted word order, with the verb before the subject.)

Where is Times Square? *Can I* get there on the subway?

Use a question mark or a period at the end of a polite request. A question mark emphasizes the politeness.

Would you please sit down?

Use a question mark with a tag question—one at the end of a sentence—even though the main clause is not a question.

This train goes to Times Square, *doesn't it*?

Use a question mark for a direct question in quotation marks, even when it is part of a declarative sentence. Put the question mark before the closing quotation mark, and use no other end punctuation.

"Have we missed the train?" she asked.

Use question marks after each question in series tag questions. (Capitalization is optional, but be consistent.)

Where did Mario go? To the library? The cafeteria? To class?

Use a question mark after a direct question enclosed within dashes.

When the phone rang—was it 7:00 A.M. already?— I jumped out of bed.

60 c Exclamation points

Use an exclamation point to convey emphasis and strong emotion in sentences that are exclamations, strong commands, or interjections.

Wow! It's late! Let's hurry!

In a direct quotation, place the exclamation point inside the quotation marks and use no other end punctuation.

"Ouch!" my brother cried. "That hurts!"

Use an exclamation point after an exclamation enclosed between dashes.

They told me—I couldn't believe it!—that I'd won.

In most college writing, use exclamation points sparingly.

61 | *Commas*

Commas are the most frequently used punctuation in English because they signal the many different ways in which sentences are divided into parts and how those parts are related, often within the same sentence.

61 a Between independent clauses

Use a comma between two or more independent clauses that are joined by words such as *for, and, nor, but, or, yet,* or *so* (coordinating conjunctions) in a compound sentence. (See Chapter 54.)

> We must act quickly, *or* the problem will get worse.

Both the comma and the coordination conjunction are necessary, unless the two sentences are very short and closely related.

> The sun rose *and* the fog lifted.

61 b After introductory elements

After an introductory element, use a comma.

> When Elizabeth I assumed the throne of England in 1558, the country was in turmoil.

> As a matter of fact, John knows the answer.

> Yes, we need to improve our parks.

However, the comma is optional if the introductory phrase is brief.

> Later the moon rose and painted the landscape silver.

If subject–verb order is inverted, no comma follows the introductory element.

> In the back of the closet⁄ was an old chest.

61 c To set off nonrestricive information

A clause essential to the meaning of a sentence is called *restrictive.* Use no commas around a restrictive clause.

> Students *who are late* will be prohibited from taking the exam.
>
> *Not all students are prohibited.*

A clause that isn't essential to meaning is called *non-restrictive.* Set it off with commas.

> Bus drivers, *who are generally underpaid,* often work long hours.
>
> *To decide, take out the clause. If the meaning is mostly un-changed (*Bus drivers often work long hours*), use commas.*

Clauses that begin with *where, which, who, whom,* or *whose* can be either restrictive or nonrestrictive. *That* is used only in restrictive clauses. *Which* is used for nonre-strictive and restrictive clauses.

RESTRICTIVE (NECESSARY: USE NO COMMAS)
The team *that* scores the most points will receive a bronze trophy.

NONRESTRICTIVE (NOT NECESSARY: USE COMMAS)
The dinner party, *which* had been carefully planned, went smoothly.

61 d Between items in a series

A series consists of three or more words or phrases. A co-ordinating conjunction—usually *and* or *or*—usually precedes the final element. Use a comma after each element in a se-ries, including the one that precedes the conjunction.

WORDS
He studied all the notes, memos, and reports.

PHRASES
To accelerate smoothly, to stop without jerking, and to make correct turns requires skill.

Be sure elements of a series are parallel in form.

> He likes skiing, surfing, and ~~to ride~~ his bicycle.
> ^riding

61 e   Between equal modifiers

Use a comma between two or more adjectives of equal weight that modify the same noun—*a warm, sunny day*. To test, try inserting *and* between them or reversing their order. If the resulting sentence still makes sense, you need a comma.

COMMAS REQUIRED

He put on a clean, pressed shirt.

He put on a pressed, clean shirt.

COMMAS NOT REQUIRED

I found five copper coins.

Five and copper coins *makes no sense.*

61 f   With parenthetical elements

A parenthetical element is a word, phrase, or clause that interrupts a sentence, but does not affect its meaning. It can appear almost anywhere in the sentence and can be moved without changing the meaning. Use commas to set off parenthetical elements.

Surprisingly enough, none of the bicycles was missing.

None of the bicycles, surprisingly enough, was missing.

None of the bicycles was missing, surprisingly enough.

61 g   Contrast, tags, and direct address

CONTRAST: Jeremiah was a bullfrog, not a toad.

TAG SENTENCE: You received my application in time, I hope.

DIRECT ADDRESS: Lilith, I hope you are well.

61 h   With quotations

Use commas to set off signal phrases that identify speakers in direct quotations. The comma appears inside the quotation marks. (See also Chapter 65.)

"When I went to kindergarten and had to speak English for the first time," writes Maxine Hong Kingston, "I became silent."

Use a question mark or an exclamation point alone, without a comma, after a quoted question or exclamation.

"What does the latest survey show?" Marion asked.

Do not use commas when preceded by *that* or with a quotation worked naturally into the sentence.

He closed by saying that time "will prove us right."

Time "will prove us right."

61 i With numbers, dates, names, and places

Counting from the right, use a comma after every three digits in numbers with five or more digits. The comma is optional in four-digit numbers.

2700 (or 2,700)   79,087   467,391

Do not use a comma in page numbers, street numbers, zip codes, or years.

21001 Southern Boulevard

Use commas before and after the year when a date giving month, day, and year is part of a sentence.

Satchmo was born on Aug. 4, 1901, in New Orleans.

When only the month and year are given or when the day precedes the month, do not use a comma.

The war broke out in August 1914 and ended on 11 November 1918.

Two commas set off a title or abbreviation following a name.

Joyce B. Wong, MD, supervised the training.

Two commas set off the name of a state following a city.

She was born in Dayton, Ohio, and stayed there.

Commas separate each element of a full address given within a sentence. The zip code does not have a comma before or after it.

Please note that my address will be 169 Elm Street, Apartment 4, Boston, MA 02116.

61   j   To prevent misreading

Even when no specific rule requires one, a comma is sometimes added to prevent misreading.

> We will all pitch in, in the event of a problem.

62 | *Semicolons*

Semicolons are used in two ways: they can join one closely related sentence to another, and they can substitute for commas in some series.

62   a   Between sentences

Use a semicolon to join two closely related sentences, especially when the second thought amplifies or contradicts the first (see 53b).

> It rained heavily in August; the leaves turned bright red in September.

> Most dogs try to please their owners; cats don't behave that way.

A semicolon may also be used with a coordinating conjunction (*and, but*) to join complex clauses, particularly when the clauses contain commas.

> If the weather clears, we'll leave at dawn; and if it doesn't, given the dangerous trail conditions, we'll pack up and go home.

62   b   Between items in a series

When at least one element of a series includes a comma, use semicolons between the elements (see 62b).

> The candidates for the award are Darnell, who won the essay competition; Elaine, the top debater; and Kiesha, the theater director.

63 | *Colons*

A colon is a more forceful stop within a sentence than a semicolon. As a mark of introduction, a colon alerts the reader that the information following it will provide further explanation. The colon also has specialized uses, such as time and biblical references.

63 a As marks of introduction

Use a colon to introduce an explanation, an example, a list, or a quotation. What precedes the colon must be a full sentence (an independent clause).

> He has but one objective: success.

> She has three objectives: money, fame, and power.

A colon may be used in place of a period or semicolon to imply that the next sentence helps make sense of the first.

> The bylaws erect a wall between the board and the director: The board sets policy, and the director implements it.

Some writers capitalize the first word after a colon when a complete sentence follows. However, a lowercase letter after a colon is always correct. Whichever you choose, be consistent.

When a full sentence precedes a quotation, use a colon.

> The song from *Porgy and Bess* puts it well: "It ain't necessarily so."

Use a colon to introduce a long quotation set off from the main text in block format (see MLA and APA guidelines).

63 b Time, citations, and titles

Hours, Minutes, and Seconds

> Court convenes at 9:00 A.M.

> The winner's time for the race was 2:45:56.

Biblical Citations

> Isaiah 14:10

In MLA style, use a period.

> Isaiah 14.10

Between Main Titles and Subtitles

> *Blue Highways: A Journey into America*

> A Deep Darkness: A Review of *Out of Africa*

Business Salutations and Memo Headings

> Dear Mr. Epstein:

> To: Alex DiGiovanni
> From: Paul Nkwami
> Subject: 2008 budget

64 | *Apostrophes*

The apostrophe appears in the possessive form of a noun, marks certain plural forms, and indicates where a letter has been dropped in contractions.

64 a   To show possession or ownership

To form the possessive case, add either an apostrophe and –*s* or just an apostrophe to nouns and some indefinite pronouns.

Singular Nouns

Use an apostrophe and –*s* to form the possessive of any noun that does not end in –*s*.

> Brad Pitt's new movie is his best yet.

Use an apostrophe and –*s* to form the possessive of a singular noun ending in –*s*. (If pronouncing the additional syllable is awkward, you may use the apostrophe alone.)

> Don't waste the class's time.

> The company produced Yeats' cycle of plays.

Plural Nouns

Use an apostrophe alone for the possessive case of a plural noun ending in *-s.*

She is managing her parents' business.

Compound Nouns

To form the possessive of a compound noun, use an apostrophe and *-s* on only the last word.

He borrowed his mother-in-law's car.

The secretary of state's office certified the results.

However, when individuals have separate possession, add an apostrophe and *-s* to each noun.

The documentary compared Aretha Franklin's and Diana Ross's early careers.

Indefinite Pronouns

Use an apostrophe to show possession with some pronouns that do not refer to any specific person or thing, such as *someone, anybody, no one, one,* and *another.*

Someone's umbrella was left at the bank.

It's no one's business but my own.

Do not use an apostrophe and *-s* with the indefinite pronouns *all, any, both, each, few, many, most, much, none, several, some,* and *such.* Use the preposition *of* to show possession with these pronouns, or use a pronoun that has a possessive form.

Let's read the works of both.

Apostrophes do not appear in the possessive forms of personal pronouns.

This book is her's.

64 b Plurals of words, letters, and symbols

Use an apostrophe to create the plural of a word discussed as a word and of a letter, number, or symbol.

There are two *perhaps*'s in that sentence.

The word occurrence is spelled with two *r*'s.

Some children have difficulty learning to write *8*'s.

Note that words, numbers, and letters referred to as themselves are italicized (or underlined). The apostrophe and the final -*s,* however, are not.

For the plurals of numbers and abbreviations, use –*s* and no apostrophe.

the 60s (or the '60s)   sixes   PhDs

Do not use an apostrophe when the century or decade is expressed in words: *the seventies.*

Use –*s* alone for abbreviations: *two MDs.*

64 c   In contractions

A contraction is a word or words with some letters intentionally omitted. An apostrophe marks the spot: *they're, 'bye.* An apostrophe also can show that digits have been dropped from a number, especially a year: *the class of '02.*

COMMON CONTRACTIONS

cannot	can't	does not	doesn't
do not	don't	would not	wouldn't
has not	hasn't	have not	haven't
will not	won't	was not	wasn't
she would	she'd	it is	it's
who is	who's	you are	you're
I am	I'm	they are	they're
let us	let's	we have	we've
there is	there's	she is	she's

65   *Quotation Marks*

Quotation marks identify words that are not your own. In writing another person's exact words, either written or spoken, you must enclose those words in quotation marks and indicate whose words they are.

Quotation marks also distinguish certain titles, foreign expressions, and special terms from the main body of the text.

Quotation style varies somewhat from discipline to discipline. This chapter follows the conventions of the Modern Language Association, the authority for papers written in the languages and literature. (See also Chapters 24–29.)

65 a   Direct quotations

When reproducing another person's exact words, keep in mind the following conventions.

Short Passages

Use quotation marks around direct quotations of up to four typed lines of prose or up to three lines of poetry. Any parenthetical citation of a source goes after the closing quotation marks but before the period.

> In *Lives under Siege*, Ratzenburger argues that "most adolescents are far too worried about the next six months and far too unconcerned about the next sixty years" (84).

American English uses double quotation marks (" ") for quotations and single quotation marks (' ')—apostrophes on the typewriter and on many computers—for quotations within quotations (or titles within titles).

> After the election, the incumbent said, "My opponent will soon learn, as someone once said, 'You can't fool all of the people all of the time.'"

Long Passages

Longer quotations should be presented in block format without quotation marks (see Chapters 26 and 31).

65 b   In dialogue

In reproducing dialogue, starting a new paragraph every time the speaker changes indicates who is speaking even without signal phrases.

> "Early parole is not the solution to overcrowding," the prosecutor said. "We need a new jail."
>
> The chairman of the county commission asked, "How do you propose we pay for it?"
>
> "Increase taxes if you must, but act quickly."

If one speaker's words continue for more than a single paragraph, use quotation marks at the beginning of each new paragraph but at the end of only the last paragraph.

65 c In certain titles

Use quotation marks for the titles of brief poems, book chapters and parts, magazine and journal articles, episodes of television series, and songs. (Use italics or underlining for titles of longer works, such as books, magazines and journals, recordings, films, plays, and television series.)

"Araby" is the third story in James Joyce's book *Dubliners*.

This chart appeared with the article "Will Your Telephone Last?" in November's *Consumer Reports*.

In my favorite episode of *I Love Lucy*, "Job Switching," Lucy and Ethel work in a chocolate factory.

Do not use quotation marks or italics for the following:

- Titles of parts of a work or series that are generic rather than specific:

  Chapter 6   Part II   Episode 43
- Titles of sacred works, parts of sacred works, and ancient manuscripts:

  the Talmud   the Bible   the Koran
- Documents:

  the Constitution   the Gettysburg Address

65 d For special purposes

Translations

Use quotation marks around the translation of a foreign word or phrase into English. The foreign word or phrase itself is italicized.

I've always called Antonio *fratellino*, or "little brother," because he is six years younger than I.

Special Terms

Use quotation marks (or italics) around specialized terms when they are first introduced and defined.

He called the new vegetable a "broccoflower," a yellow-green cross between broccoli and cauliflower.

65 e With other punctuation

Which punctuation mark comes first when a word is followed by a quotation mark and another mark of punctuation? Both logic and convention govern the order.

Periods and Commas

Put periods and commas inside quotation marks.

> After Gina finished singing "People," Joe began to hum "The Way We Were."

Colons and Semicolons

Put colons and semicolons outside quotation marks

> The sign read "Closed": there would be no soda today.

Question Marks, Exclamation Points, and Dashes

Put question marks, exclamation points, and dashes inside the quotation marks if they are part of the quotation, outside the quotation marks if they are not.

> She asked, "Have you read 'The Tiger'?"
>
> Was it you who said, "Who's there"?
>
> I can't believe you've never read "The Lottery"!
>
> Emma's first word—"Dada!"—caused Tom to beam.

66 *Other Punctuation Marks*

66 a Parentheses

Enclose elements in parentheses that would otherwise interrupt a sentence: explanations, examples, asides, and supplementary information.

- Enclose explanations, examples, and asides within a sentence.

    Relatives of famous people now famous themselves include Angelica Huston (daughter of John) and Michael Douglas (son of Kirk).

- Enclose the translation of a specialized term or foreign word that appears in italics.

    English also borrowed the Dutch word *koekje* (cookie).

- Set off the date of an event or the dates of a person's birth and death.

    The Oxford English Dictionary was first published under the editorship of James A. H. Murray (1888–1953).

- Enclose cross-references to other parts of your paper or to enclose documentation. (For more on documentation, see Parts 5–7.)

    The map (p. 4) shows the areas of heaviest rainfall.

- Enclose numbers or letters that introduce items in a list within a sentence.

    The dictionary provides (1) pronunciation, (2) etymology, (3) past meanings, and (4) usage citations for almost 300,000 words.

- Do not place a comma directly before a set of parentheses.

    His favorite author is Emily Dickinson (he refers to her as "my favorite recluse"), and he quotes her frequently.

- When a parenthetical sentence is not enclosed within another sentence, capitalize the first word and use end punctuation inside the final parenthesis.

    The countess of Dia is almost forgotten today. (She was quite well known in her time.)

- When a parenthetical sentence falls within another sentence, use no period, and do not capitalize the first word.

    Uncle Henry (he is my mother's brother) has won many awards for his charitable work.

66 b Dashes

Dashes set off explanations, definitions, examples, appositives, and other supplementary information.

> The *frijoles refritos*—refried beans—were homemade.

> We did not notice the rain—it began so softly.

Dashes indicate a pause, an interruption, or an abrupt shift in thought.

> "Well, I guess I was a little late—OK, an hour late."

> "It's exciting to see an eagle—there's one now!"

With Other Punctuation

Do not capitalize the first word enclosed by dashes within another sentence. If the enclosed sentence is a question or an exclamation, use a question mark or an exclamation point at the end, but do not capitalize the first word.

> Ward and June Cleaver—who can forget their orderly world?—never once questioned their roles in life.

Do not use commas or periods immediately before or after a dash.

Commas, Parentheses, or Dashes?

Commas, parentheses, or dashes can be used to set off non-restrictive material within a sentence (see 61c). Use commas when the material being set off is closely related in meaning to the rest of the sentence.

> A dusty plow, the kind the early Amish settlers used, hung on the wall of the old barn.

Use parentheses when the material being set off is not closely related and when you want to deemphasize it.

> Two young boys found an old plow (perhaps as old as the first Amish settlement) hidden in the barn.

Use dashes when the material being set off is not closely related to the main sentence and you want to emphasize it.

> The old plow—the one his great-grandfather had used—was still in good working order.

Dashes are flexible and frequently appear in fast, informal writing. But because speed and informality are sometimes frowned on in academic writing, use them judiciously.

66 c   Ellipsis points

Ellipsis points are three periods, each preceded and followed by a space. They are used to mark the deliberate omission of words or sentences from direct quotations.

Use an ellipsis to indicate an omission within a sentence.

> In *Drawing on the Right Side of the Brain,* Betty
> Edwards tells the reader, "You may feel that . . . it's
> the drawing that is hard."

If the omission comes before the end of a sentence in the original, use a period or other end punctuation before an ellipsis.

> Edwards says, "Drawing is not really very hard. . . .
> You may not believe me at this moment."

Use a whole line of spaced ellipsis points when you omit a line or more of poetry.

> She walks in beauty, like the night
> . . . .
> And all that's best of dark and bright
> Meet in her aspect and her eyes.

Use ellipsis points to indicate a pause or interruption in dialogue.

> "The panther tracks come from that direction . . . but
> where do they go after that?" he wondered.

66 d   Brackets

Brackets enclose words that are changed within direct quotations. If you need to make a small change that makes quoted words read correctly within the context of a sentence, enclose the change in brackets.

E. B. White writes, "Any noon in Madison Square, you may see [a sparrow] pick up a straw in his beak, [and] put on an air of great business, twisting his head and glancing at the sky."

Use the Latin word *sic* ("such") within brackets to indicate that an error in quoted material was present in the original.

In its statement, the commission said that its new health insurance program "will not effect [sic] the quality of medical care for county employees."

Within parentheses, use brackets to avoid double parentheses.

Theodore Bernstein explains that a person who feels sick is nauseated: "A person who feels sick is not nauseous any more than a person who has been poisoned is poisonous." ("Do's, Don'ts and Maybes of English Usage" [New York: New York Times, 1977]).

66 e Slashes

The slash (/) is a slanted line used to separate lines of poetry quoted in text, to indicate alternative choices, and to separate figures in certain situations.

Use a slash, preceded and followed by a space, to mark the end of a line of poetry incorporated in text.

Shakespeare opens "The Passionate Pilgrim" with a seeming paradox: "When my love swears that she is made of truth, / I do believe her, though I know she lies."

Use a slash with no space before or after to separate alternatives.

a pass/fail grading system

Use a slash to separate month, day, and year in a date given entirely in figures

7/16/99

To express a fraction in figures, use a slash between the numerator and the denominator. Use a hyphen to separate a whole number from its fraction.

5/6   2-1/16

PART twelve

Standard Writing Conventions

The conventions for **spelling** and the use of **capital letters, hyphens, italics, numbers,** and **abbreviations** help readers understand more easily.

67   *Spelling*

English spelling seems sometimes to defy reason. As the language has absorbed words from other languages, it has assumed or adapted the spellings of the originals. Pronunciation therefore is not always a good key to spelling.

67 a   Plurals

Most English plurals are made by adding *-s*. The following are exceptions to this rule.

For most nouns ending in *ch, s, sh,* or *x,* add *-es* to form the plural:

> church/churches   glass/glasses   box/boxes

For nouns ending in *y,* if the letter before the *y* is a vowel, add *-s.*

> day/days   alloy/alloys   turkey/turkeys

If the letter before the *y* is a consonant, change the *y* to *i* and add *-es.*

> melody/melodies   lady/ladies

For most nouns ending in *o,* add *-s.*

> video/videos   trio/trios   inferno/infernos

For a few nouns that end in an *o* preceded by a consonant, add *-es:*

> hero/heroes   potato/potatoes

For a few nouns that end in *o,* the plural can be formed either way.

> zero/zeros/zeroes   tornado/tornados/tornadoes

When a **compound noun** is written as one word, make only the last part of the compound plural:

> newspapers   notebooks

When a compound noun is written as separate words or hyphenated, make plural the noun that expresses the main idea:

> attorneys general   brothers-in-law   bath towels

67 b   Suffixes

A **suffix** is a letter or a group of letters added to the end of a word that changes its meaning and sometimes its spelling.

Words ending in y If the letter before the final *y* is a consonant, change the *y* to *i* before adding the suffix unless the suffix begins with *l*.

friendly/friendlier   happy/happily   apply/applying

Keep the *y* if the letter before the *y* is a vowel:

convey/conveyed   annoy/annoyed   pay/payment

Exceptions: dryly, shyly, wryly.

After words ending in e, if the suffix begins with a vowel, drop the *e*.

blue/bluer   sure/surest

When the suffix begins with a consonant, keep the final *e*.

sure/surely   polite/politeness   hate/hateful

Exceptions: *acknowledgment, argument, judgment, truly, wholly, awful,* and *ninth.*

After words ending in a consonant, do not change spelling, even if a double consonant results:

benefit/benefited   fuel/fueling   girl/girllike

The suffixes -ly or -ally turn nouns into adjectives and adjectives into adverbs.

To words that do not end in *-ic,* add *-ly.*

man/manly   absolute/absolutely   real/really

To words that end in *-ic,* Add *-ally.*

basic/basically   politic/politically

67 c   The *ie/ei* rule

The familiar rule "*i* before *e* except after *c* or when sounded like *ay* as in *neighbor* and *weigh*" holds true in most cases.

i before e: *belief, field, friend, mischief, piece, priest*
ei after c: *ceiling, conceive, deceit, deceive, receipt*
ei sounding like "ay": *eight, feign, freight, sleigh*

Exceptions:

ie after c: *ancient, conscience, science, species*

ei not after c: *caffeine, counterfeit, either, feisty, foreign, forfeit, height, leisure, neither, seize, weird*

Precede, succeed

Words with the roots *-cede, -ceed,* and *-sede* are often confused.

-cede (most common): *concede, intercede, precede*

-ceed: *exceed, proceed, succeed*

-sede (appears in only one word): *supersede*

68 *Capitalization*

C apital letters mark the beginning of sentences and the first letters of names, titles, and certain other words.

68 a The first words of sentences

Use a capital letter at the beginning of a sentence or an intentional sentence fragment. Like this.

Capitalization is optional in a series of fragmentary questions, but be consistent.

What was the occasion? A holiday? A birthday?

68 b Quotations

Capitalize the first word of quoted sentences.

"We'd like to talk to you," she said.

Do not capitalize the first word of the continuation of an interrupted quotation.

"Unfortunately," he said, "We don't sell coffee."

Lines of Poetry

Poets make deliberate decisions about when and how they use capital letters. When quoting poetry, always follow the capitalization of the original.

> Shelley's famous inscription on a shattered statue is drenched in irony: " 'My name is Ozymandias, king of kings: / Look on my works, ye Mighty, and despair.' "

68 c   Proper nouns

Capitalize the names of particular persons, places, or things:

> Mercedes Benz   Persian Gulf   Gulf of Mexico

Do not capitalize the articles, conjunctions, or prepositions that appear within such names.

Individual People and Animals

Capitalize the names and nicknames of individual people and animals:

> Ryan Howard   Chico Carrasquel   Barbaro

Capitalize words describing family members when they are used as names:

> Mother/my mother   Aunt Carol/his aunt

Religions and Their Members, Deities, and Sacred Texts

Capitalize the names of religions, members of a religion, religious sects, deities, and sacred texts:

> Judaism/Jews   Protestant   Allah   the Bible

Nationalities, Ethnic Groups, and Languages

Capitalize the names of nationalities, ethnic groups, and languages:

> French   African   American   Lithuanian

Titles of People

Capitalize formal and courtesy titles and their abbreviations when they are used before a name and not set off by commas:

> Gen. Colin Powell   Professor Cox   Ms. Wu

Titles not followed by a name when they indicate high office are usually capitlized:

the Queen   the President of the United States

Months, Days of the Week, and Holidays

Capitalize the names of months, weekdays, and holidays:

August 12, 1914   Tuesday   Labor Day

Do not capitalize numbers written out or the names of seasons:

the twentieth of April   spring

Geographic Names, Place Names, and Directions

Capitalize the names of cities, states, countries, provinces, regions, bodies of water, and other geographic features:

Little Rock, Arkansas   the Western Hemisphere

Lake Erie   the Grand Canyon   the Midwest

Capitalize direction words when they indicate regions, but not when they indicate compass directions:

the West   westerly

Institutions, Organizations, and Businesses

Capitalize the names of organizations and businesses:

Oberlin College

Federal Reserve Bank of New York

Historical Documents, Events, Periods, and Movements

Capitalize the names of historical documents and well-known events or periods:

the Constitution   the Stone Age

Movements in Art, Music, Literature, and Philosophy

Capitalize movements in the arts and philosophy:

the Enlightenment   Russian Constructionists

Ships, Aircraft, Spacecraft, and Trains

Capitalize names of individual vehicles:

Air Force One   the Titanic   the Coast Starlight

Titles

Capitalize the first word, the last word, and all other words except articles, conjunctions, and prepositions in the titles and subtitles of books, plays, essays, stories, poems, movies, television programs, pieces of music, and works of art:

Pride and Prejudice	*Beauty and the Beast*
La Traviata	"The Wasteland"
American Idol	*Guernica*

Words joined by a hyphen are usually both capitalized, except for articles, conjunctions, and prepositions:

Jack-in-the-Box

68 d   With other punctuation

Colons

When a complete sentence follows a colon, the first word may be capitalized. Be consistent.

The Senate balked at the measure: The health-care bill was dead for another decade.

Use capitals after a colon that introduces a numbered list of complete sentences (but not a list of words or phrases).

His philosophy can be reduced to three basic rules: (1) Think for yourself. (2) Take care of your body. (3) Never hurt anyone.

69 Hyphens

Hyphens link words or parts of words to create new concepts and thus new meanings. They also separate words into parts to clarify meaning or to break a word at the end of a line. In addition, hyphens have conventional uses in numbers, fractions, and units of measure.

69 a At the ends of lines

Use a hyphen to break words that are too long to fit at the end of a line. Follow these guidelines.

1. Divide words only between pronounced syllables. Words of only one pronounced syllable—*eighth, through, dreamed, urged*—should not be divided.

2. Divide at prefixes or suffixes rather than dividing base words. Try to leave both parts of a word recognizable: neither *an-tibody* nor *antibo-dy* but *anti-body;* not *ea-gerness* but *eager-ness.*

3. Don't leave just one letter at the end of a line or carry over only one or two letters to the next line.

4. A word with an internal double letter is usually divided between those letters: *syl-la-ble, wil-low,* but keep double letters together if they fall at the end of a base word, and hyphenate before a suffix: *access-ible, assess-ment, fall-ible.*

69 b After some prefixes

Use a hyphen when a prefix precedes a capitalized word or a date. The prefix itself is usually not capitalized:

pre-Columbian   pre-1994

Use a hyphen after a prefix attached to a term of two or more words:

post–World War II   anti–labor union

Use a hyphen in almost all cases after *all-, ex-, self-,* and *quasi-:*

all-inclusive   ex-convict   self-hypnosis

To prevent misreading, hyphens are often used when a prefix ends with the same letter that begins the base word:

anti-intellectual   co-ownership

Use a hyphen when two prefixes apply to the same base word. Add a space after the first hyphenated prefix.

We compared the pre- and post-election analyses.

69 c   In compound words

Many compound words are written as one word (closed compounds):

>   workhorse   schoolteacher

Other compounds are written as two separate words (open compounds):

>   hope chest   lunch break   curtain rod

But some compounds are hyphenated:

>   great-grandson   mother-in-law   stick-in-the-mud

Check the dictionary to see whether a compound is open, closed, or hyphenated. If you don't find a compound there, then it is written as two words.

Hyphenate compound nouns of three or more words:

>   jack-of-all-trades

Hyphenate when two or more modifiers act as a single adjective before a noun:

>   late-night party

Do not hyphenate well-known compound terms:

>   post office box   high school student

Do not hyphenate words ending in *-ly*:

>   a highly paid worker

69 d   Numbers, fractions, units of measure

Hyphenate two-word numbers from twenty-one to ninety-nine. Do not hyphenate before or after the words hundred, thousand, or million.

>   fifty-seven
>
>   twenty-two thousand
>
>   two hundred fifty-seven
>
>   six hundred twenty thousand

Hyphenate between the numerator and denominator of a spelled-out fraction unless one of them is already hyphenated.

>   one-half   two-thirds   twenty-one fiftieths

Hyphenate when a unit of measure is part of a modifier:

My dump truck has a nine-cubic-yard bed.

Do not hyphenate when the unit of measure is used as a noun:

My dump truck holds nine cubic yards of gravel.

Hyphenate an age whether used as a noun or a modifier:

six-year-old Robin   my son, the six-year-old

70 | *Italics*

To distinguish certain words in your text, use italics. In typewritten papers, <u>underline</u> words to indicate italics.

70 a Titles

Use italics for the titles of books, plays, operas and other long musical works, movies, recordings, newspapers, magazines, television and radio series, long poems considered to be independent works, and works of art:

Holy the Firm (book)   "Newborn and Salted" (chapter)
Leaves of Grass (book   "Song of Myself" (poem)
    of poems)
West Side Story (musical)   "Tonight" (song)
The Simpsons   "Homer Meets Godzilla"
    (television series)   (episode)

Do not use italics (or quotation marks) for titles of sacred works, parts of sacred works, ancient manuscripts, and public documents:

the Koran   the Bill of Rights   the Civil Rights Act

70 b Individual trains, ships, and planes

Italicize the official names of individual trains, ships, airplanes, and spacecraft:

City of New Orleans (train)

Spirit of St. Louis (airplane)

70 c   Foreign words

Many words of foreign origin have been absorbed into English (lasagna) and do not require italics; recently borrowed foreign words do (*pasticcio di faglioni*).

Use italics for the Latin names of plants and animals.

> *Homo erectus* is an early modern human ancestor.

Use italics for words or numbers that stand only for themselves and for letters used as symbols in mathematics and other disciplines

> the term *liberal*   to substitute *y-x* for *u*

70 d   For emphasis

Use italics to indicate that a certain word or words should receive special attention or emphasis.

> We all hear music in our heads, but how is music processed by the *brain*?

Use this kind of emphasis sparingly, as it can become monotonous.

71   *Numbers*

In writing numbers, follow the conventions of the discipline in which you are writing. For general purposes, the following guidelines will help you decide when to spell out numbers and when to use figures.

71 a   Figures or spelled-out numbers?

Spell out numbers of one hundred or less and numbers that can be expressed in one or two words:

> thirty students   three-fourths of the forest
>
> 517 students   52,331 trees

Use a combination of words and figures for round numbers over one million:

The U.S. population exceeds 250 million.

Spell out any number that begins a sentence:

Five students attended the concert.

If readers are to compare two numbers, treat them consistently:

Last year 87 cats and 114 dogs were adopted.

In technical writing, use figures for numbers over nine and in all measurements:

3 pounds per square inch

71 b Conventional uses

In all types of writing, convention requires the use of figures in certain situations.

Dates

11 April 2001   the year 1616   July 16, 2006

Addresses

2551 Polk Street, Apt. 3
San Francisco, CA 94109

With Abbreviations and Symbols

3500 rpm   37°C   65 mph $62.23   74%   53¢

If you spell out numbers, also spell out "percent," "dollars," and "cents":

seventy-four percent   fifty cents   five dollars

Time

12:15   2330 hours

Numbers used with *o'clock, past, to, till,* and *until* are generally written out as words: *seven o'clock, twenty past one.*

Decimals and Fractions

2.7 seconds   35.4 miles

Cross-References and Citations

Chapter 12   line 25   act 3, scene 2

71 c   Singular and plural forms of numbers

When the word for a number is used as a plural noun without another number before it, use the plural form of the
word. You may also need to use the word *of* after it.

The report said there were only a few protesters, but
we saw hundreds of them.

When a number appears with a unit of measure, use
the singular form for both words.

It was a ~~three-hours~~ three-hour movie.

72   *Abbreviations*

Abbreviations are frequently used in tables, footnotes,
endnotes, and bibliographies to speed up reading.

72 a   Titles and degrees

Abbreviate titles of address when they precede a full name,
except for president and mayor, which are never abbreviated. (For punctuation, see Chapter 60a.)

Mr. Samuel Taylor   Dr. Ellen Hunter

Abbreviate titles and degrees that follow a name, such
as *MD, LLD, JD,* and *PhD.* Use either a title (such as *Dr.*) or
a degree (such as *MD*), but not both.

Dr. Randall Marshall   Randall Marshall, MD

Abbreviate generational titles such as *Jr.* and *Sr.* When
used in a sentence, they are set off by commas.

He talked to Thomas Burke, Jr., and to Karen Burke.

Do not abbreviate or capitalize titles that are not used with a proper name: *assistant professor of chemistry.*

Except for *Mr., Ms., Mrs.,* and *Dr.,* do not abbreviate titles that appear before a surname alone:

U.S. Sen. Hillary Rodham Clinton   Senator Clinton

72 b   With numbers

Time

Use A.M. and P.M. (or a.m. and p.m.) for specific times of day. Capitalization is optional.

3:45 P.M. (or p.m.)   12 noon

Year

Use B.C. (before Christ) and A.D. (anno Domini) for calendar years. Only A.D. precedes the year. To avoid a religious reference, substitute B.C.E. (before the Common Era) and C.E. (Common Era).

425 B.C. (or 425 B.C.E.)   A.D. 1215 (or 1215 C.E.)

72 c   Temperature, numbers, units of measure

Use *F* for degrees Fahrenheit and *C* for degrees Celsius when writing out temperatures. Use *mph* for miles per hour. Use *no.* or *No.* for number.

Whose address is No. 10 Downing Street?

In scientific and technical writing, abbreviate units of measure, usually without periods.

He added 200 mg of sodium cyanate.

72 d   Symbols

In nontechnical writing, the symbols for degrees, percentages, and dollars may be used if quantities are expressed in numerals: *It was 30°C and sunny.*

When the numbers are written out, spell out the unit of measure as well: *We went barefoot about fifty percent of the time.*

72 e   Geographic names

Abbreviate geographic names when addressing mail. Use the U.S. Postal Service state abbreviations.

> 100 W. Glengarry Ave.
> Birmingham, MI 48009

Do not abbreviate anything but the state name when presenting a full address in text: *He lived at 11 West 6th Street, Harrisburg, PA 17102.*

Do not abbreviate state names when you give a general address: *She was born in Madison, Wisconsin.*

72 f   Common Latin abbreviations

Use common Latin abbreviations in documentation and notes, but write out their English equivalents in your text:

ABBREVIATION	LATIN	MEANING
c. or *ca.*	*circa*	*about*
cf.	*confer*	*compare*
e.g.	*exempli gratia*	*for example*
et al.	*et alii*	*and others*
etc.	*et cetera*	*and so forth*
i.e.	*id est*	*that is*
N.B.	*nota bene*	*note well*

72 g   Acronyms and initials

An *acronym* is a word made up of initials and pronounced as a word—*NATO* for North Atlantic Treaty Organization, for example. Acronyms are written with no periods and no spaces between the letters. (See 60a.)

Make sure that acronyms and initial abbreviations are familiar to your readers. If you have any doubts, give the full name the first time, followed by the abbreviation or acronym in parentheses.

> International commerce is governed by a set of treaties called the General Agreement on Tariffs and Trade (GATT).

73 | *Document Preparation*

Well-prepared documents are well received.

73 a | Preparing final copy

College instructors commonly request that academic papers follow specific style guidelines such as MLA, APA, or CMS, which are discussed in Chapters 24–38. However, if your instructor does not specify a style, follow these guidelines:

- Print on clean, white, 8½-by-11-inch paper in a readable font with one-inch margins all around.
- Double-space.
- Include name, course title, instructor name, and date on the first page, flush with the upper left-hand margin. Double-space.
- Center the title on the next line, using initial capital letters for all main words. Double-space.
- Indent the first word of each paragraph five spaces.
- Space once after each word and after each sentence.
- Set off quotations of four lines or more in double-spaced block format, indented ten spaces.
- Number each page in the upper right-hand corner, one-half inch from the top, unless otherwise instructed.
- As protection against separated pages, include your last name or an abbreviated title before each page number.

73 b | Proofreading

Proofreading is the process of finding and correcting errors in typing, spelling, punctuation, and mechanics. Plan to proofread twice: once on the edited draft from which you will prepare your final copy and once on the final copy itself.

- Make a printout. Shifting from computer screen to paper makes it easier to spot errors.

- Read your writing aloud. Listen for anything that isn't clear and natural.

- Ask someone else to proofread your final draft.

- Read backward, starting with the last word and work back, one word at a time, to the first, using a ruler to focus on one line at a time.

- Use your computer's spell checker, but note that spell checkers do not catch wrong or omitted words.

- Use standard proofreading symbols (inside back cover) to mark corrections.

- Make corrections on the electronic text and reprint.

This glossary provides information about frequently confused, misused, and nonstandard words. It also lists colloquial usages that are common in informal writing, but often unacceptable in academic writing.

a, an   Use *a* before words that begin with a consonant sound (*a* boy, *a* history), even if the first letter of the word is a vowel (*a* useful lesson). Use *an* before words that begin with a vowel sound (*an* antelope, *an* hour).

accept, except   *Accept* is a verb meaning "to receive" or "to approve" (*I accept your offer*). *Except* is usually a preposition meaning "excluding" (*He liked to eat everything except vegetables*).

adapt, adopt   *Adapt* means "to adjust" or "to accommodate"; it is usually followed by *to* (*It is sometimes hard to adapt to college life*). *Adopt* means "to take and use as one's own" (*My parents are adopting another child*).

advice, advise   *Advice* is a noun; *advise* is a verb. *I advise you to take my advice and study hard.*

affect, effect   *Affect* as a verb means "to influence" or "to produce an effect" (*That movie affected me deeply*). *Effect* is commonly used as a noun meaning "result." (*That movie had a profound effect on me*). *Effect* can also be a verb meaning "to bring about" (*Dr. Jones effected important changes as president*).

all ready, already   *All ready* means "fully prepared" (*The children were all ready for bed*). *Already* means "previously" (*The children were already in bed when I arrived*).

all right, alright   *All right* is always written as two words. *Alright* is nonstandard.

all together, altogether   *All together* means "all gathered in one place" (*The animals were all together in the ark*). *Altogether* means "thoroughly" or "completely" (*The ark was altogether too full of animals*).

allusion, illusion *Allusion* means "an indirect reference"; an illusion is a misconception or false impression. (*The movie had many allusions to Shakespeare. Mr. Hodges created an optical illusion with two lines*).

a lot *A lot* should always be written as two words.

among, between Use *among* with three or more individuals, *between* with two. (*It was difficult to choose among all the exotic plants. There were significant differences between the two orchids*).

amount, number Use *amount* with quantities that cannot be counted; use *number* with those that can. (*It took a great amount of paint to fix up the farmhouse. A large number of volunteers showed up to clean out the building*).

anxious, eager *Anxious* is an adjective meaning "worried" or "uneasy." Do not confuse it with *eager,* which means "enthusiastic." (*Lynn is anxious about the surgery.*)

as *As* may be used to mean "because" (*We did not go ice skating as the lake was no longer frozen*), but only if there is no ambiguity. (*We canceled the meeting because* [not as] *only two people showed up.*)

as, as if, like To indicate comparisons, *like* should be used only as a preposition to compare items (*Ken, like his brother, prefers to sleep late*). Avoid using *like* as a conjunction linking two clauses. Use *as* or *as if* instead (*Anne talks as if* [not like] *she has read every book by Ernest Hemingway*).

awful, awfully *Awful* is an adjective meaning "inspiring awe." In formal writing, do not use it to mean "disagreeable" or "objectionable." The adverb *awfully* means "in an awe-inspiring way"; avoid using it in the colloquial sense of "very."

awhile, a while The one-word form *awhile* is an adverb that can be used to modify a verb (*We rested awhile*). Only the two-word form *a while* can be the object of a preposition (*We rested for a while*).

bad, badly *Bad* is an adjective, so it must modify a noun or follow a linking verb, such as *be, feel,* or *become* (*John felt bad about holding the picnic in bad weather*).

Badly is an adverb, so it must modify a verb (*Pam played badly today*).

beside, besides   *Beside* is a preposition meaning "by the side of" or "next to" (*The book is beside the bed*). *Besides* can be used as a preposition meaning "other than" or "in addition to" (*No one besides Linda can build a good campfire*). *Besides* is also an adverb meaning "furthermore" or "in addition" (*The weather is bad for hiking; besides, I have a cold*).

between   See *among, between.*

bring, take   The verb *bring* describes movement from a distant place to a nearer place; the verb *take* describes movement away from a place (*Dr. Gavin asked us to bring our rough sketches to class; she said we may take them home after class*).

can, may   Traditionally *can* is used to indicate ability, and *may* indicates permission. (*I can see much better with my new glasses. May I borrow your dictionary?*)

capital, capitol   *Capital* refers to a city, *capitol* to a building where lawmakers meet. (*Albany is the capital of New York. The civics class toured the state capitol last week*). *Capital* also means "accumulated wealth."

cite, sight, site   *Cite* means "to quote for purposes of example, authority, or proof" (*Tracy cites several legal experts in her paper on capital punishment*). *Sight* refers to vision. *Site* means "place or scene" (*Today we poured the foundation on the site of our future home*). Pages on the Internet are referred to as *sites*.

complement, compliment   *Complement* is a verb meaning "to fill out or complete" or a noun meaning "something that completes or fits with" (*The bouquet of spring flowers complemented the table setting*). *Compliment* is a verb meaning "to express esteem or admiration" or a noun meaning "an expression of esteem or admiration" (*Russ complimented Nancy on her choice of flowers*). As a noun, *compliment* means a flattering remark or action (*The team voted her captain, which she took as a compliment*).

conscience, conscious   *Conscience* is a noun referring to a sense of right and wrong (*His conscience would not* *allow him to lie). Conscious* is an adjective meaning "marked by thought or will" or "acting with critical awareness" (*He made a <u>conscious</u> decision to be honest*).

continual, continuous *Continual* means "occurring repeatedly" (*Liz saw a doctor about her <u>continual</u> headaches*). *Continuous* means "uninterrupted in space, time, or sequence" (*Eventually we grew used to the <u>continuous</u> noise*).

council, counsel *Council* is a noun meaning "a group meeting for advice, discussion, or government" (*The tribal <u>council</u> voted in favor of the new land-rights law*). *Counsel* is a noun meaning "advice" (*The priest gave <u>counsel</u> to the young men considering the priesthood*). It can also refer to a legal representative. *Counsel* as a verb means "to advise."

criteria, criterion *Criteria* is the plural of *criterion,* which means "a standard on which a judgment is based" (*Many <u>criteria</u> are used in selecting a president, but a candidate's hair color is not an appropriate <u>criterion</u>*).

data *Data* is the plural of *datum,* which means "an observed fact." But *data* is increasingly being used as a singular noun (*The <u>data</u> indicate* [or *indicates*] *that a low-fat diet may increase life expectancy*). The singular *datum* is rarely used.

defuse, diffuse *Defuse* means literally to remove a fuse, or, in a figurative sense, to calm a potentially explosive situation. *Diffuse* means "to spread out" or, as an adjective, "spread out, not concentrated."

different from, different than *Different from* is preferred to *different than* (*Hal's taste in music is <u>different from</u> his wife's*). But *different than* may be used to avoid awkward constructions (*Hal's taste in music is <u>different than</u>* [instead of *different from what*] *it was five years ago*).

disinterested, uninterested *Disinterested* is an adjective meaning "unbiased" (*It will be difficult to find twelve <u>disinterested</u> jurors*). *Uninterested* is an adjective meaning "indifferent" or "unconcerned" (*Most people were <u>uninterested</u> in the case until the police discovered surprising new evidence*).

enthused, enthusiastic   As an adjective, enthusiastic is preferred (*Barbara is <u>enthusiastic</u>* [not *enthused*] *about her music lessons*).

etc.   Avoid ending a list with *etc.;* indicate that you are leaving items out of a list with *and so on* or *and so forth.*

everybody, everyone, every one   *Everybody* and *everyone* are singular indefinite pronouns that refer to an unspecified person (*<u>Everybody</u> wins in this game*). The phrase *every one* refers to each individual member of a group (*<u>Every one</u> of these toys is to be picked up*).

except   See *accept, except.*

farther, further   Use *farther* to refer to physical distances (*Boston is <u>farther</u> than I thought*) and *further* to refer to quantity, time, or degree (*We made <u>further</u> progress on our research project*).

fewer, less   *Fewer* refers to people or items that can be counted; *less* refers to general amounts. (*<u>Fewer</u> people went to the conference this year. We needed <u>less</u> space.*)

firstly, secondly, thirdly   These expressions are awkward; use *first, second,* and *third.*

good, well   *Good* is an adjective; it should not be used in place of the adverb *well* in formal writing (*Mario is a <u>good</u> tennis player; he played <u>well</u>* [not *good*] *today*).

hardly, scarcely   Avoid phrases like *can't scarcely* and *not hardly* in formal writing; these are double negatives (*I can <u>scarcely</u>* [not *can't scarcely*] *keep my eyes open*).

he or she, his or her   Use *he or she* and *his or her* to keep language gender neutral. (See 56c.)

hopefully   *Hopefully* is an adverb meaning "in a hopeful manner" (*The child looked <u>hopefully</u> out the window for her mother*). In formal writing, do not use *hopefully* to mean "I hope that" or "It is hoped that" (*I <u>hope that</u>* [not *Hopefully*] *Bob will remember his camera*).

illusion   See *allusion, illusion.*

imply, infer   *Imply* means "to express indirectly" or "to suggest"; *infer* means "to conclude" (*Helen implied that she had time to visit with us, but we inferred from all the work on her desk that she was really too busy*). A speaker *implies*; a listener *infers*.

irregardless, regardless   Do not use the nonstandard *irregardless* in place of *regardless* (*We will have the party regardless [not irregardless] of the weather*).

its, it's   *Its* is a possessive pronoun; *it's* is a contraction for *it is* (*It's almost noon*).

kind of, sort of   Avoid using the colloquial expressions *kind of* and *sort of* to mean "somewhat" or "rather" (*My paper is rather [not kind of] short; my research for it was somewhat [not sort of] rushed*).

lay   See *lie, lay*.

lead, led   As a verb, *lead* rhymes with "deed" and means "to go first" or "to direct"; as a noun, it means "front position" (*Jill will take the lead*). The noun *lead*, referring to a metal, is pronounced like *led*. *Led* is the past tense and past participle of the verb *lead* (*He led us to the cave*).

learn, teach   *Learn* means "to gain knowledge or understanding"; *teach* means "to cause to know" or "to instruct" (*Tonight Jim will teach [not learn] us a new dance.*)

less   See *fewer, less*.

lie, lay   Lie is a verb meaning "to recline" or "to rest in a horizontal position." Its forms are *lie, lay, lain*. *Lay* is a transitive verb (followed by a direct object) meaning "to put or set down." Its forms are *lay, lie, laid*. (*Lay the blanket on this spot and lie [not lay] down.*)

like   See *as, as if, like*.

loose, lose   *Loose* is an adjective meaning "not securely attached." *Lose* is a verb that means "to misplace" or "to undergo defeat" (*Be careful not to lose that loose button on your jacket*).

may   See *can, may*.

may be, maybe   *May be* is a verb phrase (*Charles may be interested in a new job*); *maybe* is an adverb meaning "possibly" (*Maybe I will speak to him about it*).

media   *Media* is the plural of *medium* (*Some people felt that the media were* [not *was*] *responsible for the candidate's loss*).

moral, morale   *Moral* is the lesson of a story or experience (*The moral is to treat others as you wish to be treated*). *Morale* is the mental condition or mood of a person or group (*The good weather lifted the crew's morale*).

most   Avoid using *most* to mean "almost" (*Prizes were given to almost* [not *most*] *all the participants*).

myself   *Myself* is a reflexive or intensive pronoun. Reflexive: *I hurt myself.* Intensive: *I will do it myself.* Do not use *myself* in place of *I* or *me*: *She gave the food to Jill and me* [not *myself*].

number   See *amount, number*.

of   See *have, of*.

passed, past   *Passed* is the past-tense form of the verb *pass* (*She passed here several hours ago*). *Past* may be an adjective or a noun referring to a time before the present (*She told stories about the distant past*).

perspective, prospective   *Perspective* is a noun meaning "a point of view"; do not confuse it with the adjective *prospective* meaning "potential" or "likely" (*Mr. Harris's perspective on the new school changed when he met his son's prospective teacher*).

precede, proceed   *Precede* means "to come before"; *proceed* means "to go forward" (*The bridal attendants preceded the bride into the church; when the music started, they proceeded down the aisle*).

principal, principle   *Principal* is a noun meaning "head of a school or organization" or "an amount of money." It is also an adjective meaning "most important." *Principle* is a noun meaning "a rule of action" or "a basic law" (*My high school principal suggested a trip to Gettysburg. My principal reason for going was my* *interest in the Civil War, but I also wanted to learn about the <u>principles</u> of the U.S. Constitution).*

quotation, quote   *Quotation* is a noun, and *quote* is a verb. Avoid using *quote* as a noun (*Sue <u>quoted</u> Jefferson in her speech, hoping the <u>quotation</u> [not quote] would have a powerful effect on her audience*).

real, really   *Real* is an adjective; *really* is an adverb. Avoid using *real* as an adverb (*Tim was <u>really</u> [not real] interested in buying Lana's old car*).

reason why   *Reason why* is redundant. (*The <u>reason</u> [not The reason why] we canceled the meeting is that no one came*).

respectfully, respectively   *Respectfully* means "in a respectful manner" (*The children listened to their teacher <u>respectfully</u>*). *Respectively* means "in the order given" (*The sessions on Italian, French, and Spanish culture are scheduled for Tuesday, Wednesday, and Thursday <u>respectively</u>*).

sensual, sensuous   *Sensual* means "arousing the senses or appetites" and often refers to sexual pleasure (*His scripts often featured <u>sensual</u> encounters*). *Sensuous* means "pleasing to the senses" and refers to aesthetic enjoyment (*Her sculpture was characterized by muted colors and <u>sensuous</u> curves*).

set, sit   *Set* means "to put" or "to place"; *sit* means "to be seated." (*Mary <u>set</u> her packages on the kitchen table. I <u>sat</u> in the only chair in the waiting room*).

sight   See *cited, sight, site.*

since   Do not use *since* to mean "because" when there is any chance of ambiguity. *<u>Because</u> [not since] she sold her bicycle, Lonnie has not been getting much exercise. Since* here could mean either "because" or "from the time that."

sit   See *set, sit.*

site   See *cite, sight, site.*

somebody, someone, something   These singular indefinite pronouns take singular verbs (*<u>Someone</u> calls every night at midnight and hangs up*).

sure, surely Avoid using the adjective *sure* to mean "certainly"; use *surely* or *certainly* instead (*It certainly* [or *surely*; not *sure*] *is cold today*).

take See *bring, take.*

than, then *Than* is a conjunction used in comparisons (*Dan is older than Eve*). *Then* is an adverb indicating time (*First pick up the files and then deliver them to the company office*).

that, which Many writers reserve *that* for restrictive clauses, *which* for nonrestrictive clauses. (See 61c.)

their, there, they're *Their* is the possessive form of the pronoun *they* (*Did they leave their books here?*). *There* is an adverb meaning "in or at that place" (*No, they left their books there*). *They're* is a contraction of *they are* (*They're looking all over for their books*).

then See *than, then.*

to, too, two *To* is a preposition used to indicate movement or direction toward something (*Nancy is walking to the grocery store*). *Too* is an adverb meaning "also" (*Sam is walking too*). *Two* is a number (*The two of them are walking together*).

utilize The verb *utilize* means "to put to use." It often sounds pretentious; *use* is sufficient. (*We were able to use* [not *utilize*] *the hotel kitchen to prepare our meals*).

wait for, wait on *Wait for* means "to await" or "to be ready for." *Wait on* means "to serve" (*You are too old to wait for* [not *on*] *your mother to wait on you*).

way, ways Do not use *ways* in place of *way* when referring to long distances (*Los Angeles is a long way* [not *ways*] *from San Francisco*).

well See *good, well.*

where *Where* is nonstandard when used in place of *that* (*I read that* [not *where*] *several of the factories will close soon*).

whether, weather *Whether* is a conjunction referring to a choice between alternatives; the noun *weather* refers to the state of the atmosphere. (*Mike wondered whether the weather would clear up for the game.*)

which, who, that Use *which* to refer to places, things, or events; use *who* to refer to people. Use *that* to refer to things or, occasionally, to a group or class of people. (*The parade, <u>which</u> was rescheduled for Saturday, was a great success. The man <u>who</u> [not which] was grand marshal said it was the best parade <u>that</u> he could remember.*)

while See *although, while.*

who, whom Use *who* for subjects and subject complements; use *whom* for objects and object complements (<u>*Who*</u> *revealed the murderer's identity?*). (See 56d).

who's, whose *Who's* is a contraction of *who is* (<u>*Who's*</u> *coming for dinner tonight?*). *Whose* is the possessive form of *who* (<u>*Whose*</u> *hat is lying on the table?*).

your, you're *Your* is the possessive form of the pronoun *you* (<u>*Your*</u> *table is ready*); *you're* is a contraction of *you are* (<u>*You're*</u> *leaving before the end of the show?*).

GLOSSARY

of Grammatical Terms

Active vs. passive voice   When a verb is in the active voice, the subject of the sentence does the action. *Mary caught the ball.* In the passive voice, the subject becomes the agent of the action: *The ball was caught by Mary.* Sometimes the agent does not appear in the passive-voice sentence: *The ball was caught.* (See 54h.)

Adjective   A word that modifies (describes) the meaning of nouns, pronouns, or phrases and clauses used as nouns. *Those are scarlet tanagers* (modifies noun *tanagers*). *They were beautiful* (modifies pronoun *they*). *To see them would be delightful* (modifies phrase *to see them*). (See Chapter 57.)

Adverb   A word that modifies verbs, adjectives, or other adverbs; they can also modify clauses or entire sentences. *His judgment was made hastily* (modifies verb *was made*). *The feathers are quite beautiful* (modifies adjective *beautiful*). (See Chapter 57.)

Agreement   Matching in person, case, or number. (See Chapter 55 and 56b.)

Antecedent   The word to which a pronoun refers: *The dog who barked came into the house. Who* refers back to *dog.* (See 56a.)

Appositive   A phrase that appears directly after a noun or pronoun and renames or further identifies it: *Ralph Nader, a longtime consumer advocate, supports auto emission controls.* (See 56c.)

Article   The words *a, an, the,* used to mark a noun. (See 59a.)

Auxiliary verb   A verb used with a main verb: *be, am, is, are, was, were, being, been; has, have, had; do, does, did; can, will, shall, should, could, would, may, might, must.* A helping verb always comes before a main verb: *will sing, could sing, is singing, had sung.* (See 54d.)

Case   Subjective case is used for subjects; possessive case shows ownership; objective case is used for the recipient of an action. See 56c.

Clause   Any group of related words with a subject (usually a noun or pronoun) and a predicate (a verb) is a clause. A clause that can stand alone as a complete sentence is called an **independent clause:** *The moon rose.* A clause that cannot stand by itself as a complete sentence is called a **dependent clause** and must be joined to an independent clause: *The clouds parted <u>when the moon rose</u>.* (See Chapter 46.)

Complement   See *object complement, subject complement.*

Complex sentence   A sentence with one independent clause and at least one dependent clause. In the following example, the dependent clause is underlined: *The students assemble outside <u>when the bell rings</u>.*

Compound-complex sentence   A sentence containing at least two independent clauses and at least one dependent clause. In the following example, the dependent clause is underlined: *The first motorcyclists to arrive never ordered anything to eat; they just sat quietly <u>until their hands stopped shaking</u>.*

Compound sentence   A sentence consisting of two or more independent clauses, usually joined by a comma or *for, and, nor, but, or, yet, <u>so</u>* (coordinating conjunction): *They grew tired of waiting, <u>so</u> they finally hailed a taxi.* (See 46a and Chapter 53.)

Conjunction   A word that joins two or more words, phrases, or clauses. The **coordinating conjunctions**—*for, and, nor, but, or, yet,* and *so*—imply that the elements linked are equal or similar in importance. *Bill <u>and</u> I went shopping. The bus will take you to the market <u>or</u> to the theater.*

Correlative conjunction   A word pair that connects similar words, phrases, or clauses: *either . . . or, neither . . . nor, both . . . and, not only . . . but also, whether . . .or.* *<u>Neither</u> Jack <u>nor</u> his brother was home. She <u>not only</u> sings <u>but</u> dances.*

Demonstrative pronoun   A pronoun such as *this, that, these,* and *those,* used to identify a specific person, place, or thing: *<u>This</u> is the largest one we have.*

Dependent clause   See *clause.*

Direct object A word that receives the action of a transitive verb: *The company paid its <u>workers</u> a day early.* The direct object <u>workers</u> receives the action of *paid*.

Gerund A verb form ending in *-ing* (the present participle) used as a noun: <u>*Swimming*</u> *is fun.*

Helping verb See *auxiliary verb.*

Indefinite pronoun A pronoun that does not refer to any specific person, animal, place, thing, or idea: *anyone, everybody, something, many, few,* and *none*. <u>*Many*</u> *are called, but <u>few</u> are chosen.* (See 55e and 56b.)

Independent clause See *clause.*

Indirect object A person or thing to whom (or for whom) the action of the verb is directed: *Ben Rothlisberger threw <u>Hines Ward</u> the football.*

Infinitive The base form of a verb, preceded by *to: to sing, to walk.*

Interjection A word that shows surprise, dismay, or strong emotion, often appearing in speech or dialogue and usually taking an exclamation point. <u>*Ouch!*</u> *That pipe is hot!*

Interrogative pronoun One used to ask questions: *who, what, which, whose.* <u>*Who*</u> *is there?* <u>*Whose*</u> *footsteps did I hear?*

Intransitive verb See *transitive and intransitive verbs.*

Irregular verb (See *regular and irregular verbs* and 54a and 54b.)

Linking verb A verb that connects the subject to a word that renames or modifies it: *be, become, seem,* and verbs describing sensations: *appear, look, feel, taste, smell,* and *sound.* For example, *The flowers are fragrant. (flowers = fragrant).* (See 54d and 56c.)

Modifier A word, phrase, or clause that describes or qualifies the meaning of a another word. (See *adjective* and *adverb* and Chapter 57.)

Mood The property of a verb that expresses the speaker's attitude toward or relation to the action. The three moods in English are (1) <u>indicative</u> (facts, opinions, questions): *It is cold.* (2) <u>imperative</u> (commands or directives): *Stop!* and (3) <u>subjunctive</u> (wishes, requirements, or conditions contrary to fact): *I wish it <u>were</u> warmer.* (See 54g.)

Noun   A word that names a person, place, thing, or concept: *woman, dog, canyon, vase, virtue.* A **proper noun** names a particular person or thing: *Marie Curie, Kentucky, Porsche, Catholicism.* Proper nouns are capitalized. A **common noun** applies to any member of a class or group: *scientist, horse, state, ship, religion.* A **count noun** refers to one or more individual items that can readily be counted: *one book, two books.* A **noncount noun** refers to entities that cannot be counted individually—*water, oil.* A **collective noun** refers to groups—*crowd, couple,* and *flock*—and may be singular or plural. (See 55d.) A **possessive noun** indicates ownership with an apostrophe and an *-s: John's book.*

Object   See *direct object, indirect object.*

Object complement   A word or word group that renames or describes a direct object. It always comes after the direct object: *Tonight we will name him chairman.* The adjective *chairman* renames the direct object *him.*

Participle, past   One of the five verb forms: *walked, chosen, broken.* (See 54a.) To be the main verb of a sentence, a past participle requires an auxiliary verb (*has chosen*), but a past participle may also be used as a modifier (*freshly <u>baked</u> bread*).

Participle, present   One of the five verb forms, ending in *-ing,* used with an auxiliary verb to form a main verb (*is <u>going</u>*). Can be used as an adjective (*an <u>aging</u> population*) or a noun (*I like <u>skiing</u>*). (See 54a.)

Parts of speech   A system for classifying words by grammatical type: *Nouns, pronouns, verbs, adjectives, adverbs, prepositions, conjunctions,* and *interjections* are parts of speech.

Passive voice   See *active vs. passive voice.*

Personal pronoun   A word used to refer to a specific person, place, or thing: *I, me, you, she, her, he, him, their, it.* For example: *I asked <u>you</u> to buy <u>it</u>.* (See Chapter 56.)

Phrase   A group of related words that lacks either a subject or predicate or both. See *prepositional phrase, verb phrase.*

Possessive pronoun   A pronoun that shows ownership: *my, mine, your, yours, her, hers, his, its, our, ours, your, yours, their, theirs.* For example: *I lent her <u>my</u> books.* (See Chapter 56c.)

Predicate   The verb of a sentence, along with objects, modifiers, or complements: *A woman in a yellow raincoat <u>ran to catch the bus</u>.* The **simple predicate** is the main verb of the sentence: *ran.*

Preposition   A word that shows a relationship between a noun or pronoun and other words in the sentence. Common prepositions include *about, above, across, after, around, at, before, behind, below, beside, between, beyond, by, down, during, of, over, since, through, toward, under, upon,* and *with.* (See 59c.)

Prepositional phrase   A phrase consisting of a preposition, its object, and any related modifiers: *The new book was hailed <u>with great fanfare</u>.* (See 59c.)

Pronoun   A word that substitutes for a noun. The word the pronoun replaces comes before the pronoun and is called its **antecedent.** A pronoun must agree with its antecedent in terms of person, number, and gender. *Sean helped <u>Alicia</u> paint <u>her</u> room. Alicia* is the antecedent of the pronoun *her.* See also *demonstrative pronoun, indefinite pronoun, intensive or reflexive pronoun, interrogative pronoun, personal pronoun, relative pronoun.* (See Chapter 56.)

Reflexive and intensive pronoun   A pronoun ending in *-self* or *-selves* that refers back to the subject: *myself, yourself, themselves: Dave cut <u>himself</u> while shaving.* Called an *intensive* pronoun when it emphasizes or "intensifies": *I talked to the president <u>herself</u>.*

Regular, irregular verbs   A regular verb forms the past tense and the past participle by adding *-ed* or *-d* to the base: *talk, talked.* Irregular verbs don't follow that pattern: *sing, sang, sung; take, took, taken; begin, began, begun.* (See 54a and 54b.)

Relative adverb   *When* or *where,* used to introduce a dependent clause. *The book will be available <u>when you return.</u>*

Relative pronoun A pronoun such as *who, whom, whoever, which, whichever, that, what, whatever* that introduces a dependent clause. *She chose the knife <u>that</u> was the sharpest.*

Sentence A word group consisting of at least one independent clause: a subject (e.g., noun/pronoun) and a predicate (e.g., verb). See also *simple sentence, compound sentence, complex sentence, compound-complex sentence.* (See Chapters 52 and 53.)

Simple sentence A sentence consisting of a single independent clause (subject and predicate) and no subordinate clause: *John ran. Monkeys eat bananas.*

Subject The subject performs the action of the sentence. The subject usually comes at the beginning of a sentence: *A <u>woman in a yellow raincoat</u> ran to catch the bus.* The **simple subject** of a sentence is the person or thing that performs the action of the predicate: *<u>John</u> ran.* A **compound subject** includes two or more subjects linked by a coordinating conjunction: *<u>Books, records, and videotapes</u> filled the room.*

Subject complement A word that renames or describes the subject of a sentence. It follows a *linking verb* (*be, become, seem,* or *appear;* see 54d). Whatever appears before the linking verb is the subject; what appears after is the subject complement: *My mother's <u>uncle</u> is the factory <u>foreman</u>.* (See 54d.)

Subjunctive mood A mood used to express wishes, requests, recommendations, and conditions contrary to fact. *I would be happier if you were here.* (See 54g.)

Subordinating conjunction A word that introduces a dependent (subordinate) clause: *<u>After</u> we arrive, we will eat.* (See 46b, 53d.)

Transitive and intransitive verbs A transitive verb takes a direct object (receives the action): *Joey <u>grew</u> tomatoes last summer.* An intransitive verb does not take a direct object: *Sheila <u>slept</u>.* (See 54d.)

Verbal A verb form that does not change form to show person or number. An *infinitive* is the base form of the verb, usually preceded by the word *to* (*to visit*). (After certain verbs, the *to* of an infinitive disappears: *She let them visit their cousins.*) A *gerund* is the *-ing* form of the verb used as a noun (*visiting*). The past participle, usually ending in *-ed* or *-d* (*visited*), and the present participle, ending in -ing (*visiting*), can be used as modifiers.

Verb phrase   The main verb and its auxiliaries: *The college has been having a difficult year.* (See 54d.)

Verb   A verb conveys an action (*The logger fells the tree*) or a state of being (*The air is fragrant*). The verb of a sentence changes form to show *person, number, tense, voice,* and *mood.* (See Chapters 48 and 54.)

Voice   See *active vs. passive voice.*

PHOTO CREDITS

INDEX

Notes

Notes

Notes

Notes

Notes

Before Baby Arrives

A Mother's
Pregnancy Journal

*D*ear Mother-to-Be,

You are about to embark on one of the most incredible journeys of your life!

From this day forward, much of your life will revolve around a small human being who will steal your heart long before entering the world. You will have strangers patting your stomach, offering you advice (whether you ask for it or not), and well-meaning friends who can only recall (unfortunately) the most sordid of childbearing tales. Your body will grow, your heart will be filled, your life will be changed...forever.

Little things will mean so much...like the first time you hear your baby's heartbeat and feel the flutters and undeniable movement of your child snuggled inside. No one can tell you, convince you, describe to you...the incredible experience of bringing a new life into this world.

For the next nine months, you will make a new discovery every day. You will record, in this journal, the moments you'll cherish forever and want to share with your child in later years.

Your next months will be filled with a variety of activities. You will be decorating the nursery, picking names for the baby, choosing a pediatrician, learning more than you ever expected to know about childbirth, and visiting your doctor on a regular basis. The day you so anticipate will arrive quickly...but you will be prepared.

And before you know it, instead of talking about due dates, you'll be talking about birthdays and labor and how you never realized how much love you could feel for one tiny person. And you'll never forget how magically wonderful this journey has been, this miracle of motherhood.

Welcome, little one.
Strong arms will hold you.
Caring hearts will tend you.
Love awaits you...

This pregnancy journal
has been completed by

_____

for my child

_____

To the little one I began to love
long before I saw your face,
before I knew your name,
before I could hold you in my arms...
to my child, my miracle.

L is for the Laughter
and the love as baby grows,

O is for the little One
your heart already knows,

V is for the Very special someone
you'll soon see,

E is for Each fun-filled day
of new discovery!

The First Three Months

You came into my life in a very special way. I
knew something was different. My body told me
my life was about to change. I felt _____

_____

_____

_____

_____

_____

_____

I knew for certain I was pregnant on _____

_____

when _____

_____

_____

_____

_____

_____

I could hardly wait to tell someone about my pregnancy. I wanted to call others to share my news. The first person I told was _____.
Date and reaction to the news: _____

_____

_____

_____

_____

_____

_____

_____

_____

_____

_____

_____

_____

_____

_____

_____

_____

_____

Others who heard my exciting news were _____

This was a very special time for me. Some of my
thoughts and feelings were _____

_____

_____

_____

_____

_____

_____

_____

_____

_____

_____

_____

_____

_____

_____

_____

_____

_____

_____

_____

Choosing a doctor/medical caregiver to take care of us and help bring you into the world was important. I chose _____

because _____

_____

_____

_____

_____

_____

_____

_____

_____

_____

_____

The office was located at _____

_____.

I will go there many times before you arrive. My first appointment was on _____

_____.

And here is a photo of how I looked as we began this adventure.

I gained

_____ pounds by the end of the first month.

_____ pounds by the end of the second month.

_____ pounds by the end of the third month.

The foods I crave are _____

_____

_____

_____

_____

_____

_____

_____

_____

_____

_____

_____

_____

_____

_____

Instructions and advice the doctor/medical caregiver gave me during my first visit were

_____

_____

_____

_____

_____

_____

_____

_____

_____

_____

_____

_____

_____

_____

_____

_____

_____

_____

_____

I was also told that your arrival date would be
about _____.
Some other things I wanted to discuss with my
doctor/medical caregiver were _____

_____

_____

_____

_____

_____

_____

_____

_____

_____

_____

_____

_____

_____

_____

_____

_____

I decided that your place of arrival would be at

_____

It was located at _____

I chose it because _____

_____

_____

_____

_____

_____

_____

_____

_____

_____

_____

_____

_____

_____

_____

_____

When I try to imagine what it will be like to go there for your birth, I expect _____

_____

_____

_____

_____

_____

_____

_____

_____

_____

_____

_____

_____

_____

_____

_____

_____

_____

_____

_____

_____

Already I wonder what you will look like and what kind of person you will be. I share my thoughts with you, wondering if you can hear me. I wonder if you already know how very much you are loved. I have so many hopes for you:

_____

_____

_____

_____

_____

_____

_____

_____

_____

_____

_____

_____

_____

_____

_____

_____

I wonder about family traits you might inherit:

_____
_____
_____
_____
_____
_____
_____
_____

And there are some family traits I hope you
won't inherit: _____

_____
_____
_____
_____
_____
_____
_____
_____

I would like for you to know all that is happening in my life now. Here are some of the things I am thinking and doing while waiting for you to be born: _____

_____

_____

_____

_____

_____

_____

_____

_____

_____

_____

_____

_____

_____

_____

_____

_____

_____

_____

Jobs I held outside the home: _____

_____

_____

_____

_____

Classes I took: _____

_____

_____

_____

_____

Events I attended: _____

_____

_____

_____

_____

Exercise routine: _____

_____

_____

Other: _____

_____

How can the anticipation of one small child
change my world so completely? My special
memories of these first months of expecting you
are _____

_____

_____

_____

_____

_____

_____

_____

_____

_____

_____

_____

_____

_____

_____

_____

_____

_____

My most noticeable physical changes so far have
been _____

_____

_____

_____

_____

_____

_____

_____

As far as my general health, I _____

_____

_____

_____

_____

_____

_____

_____

_____

The Second Three Months

Even though there are six more months of waiting, I already think about what it will be like when you arrive. Some of my thoughts are

_____

_____

_____

_____

_____

_____

_____

_____

_____

_____

_____

_____

_____

_____

_____

_____

_____

_____

I gained

_____ pounds by the end of the fourth month.

_____ pounds by the end of the fifth month.

_____ pounds by the end of the sixth month.

The foods I crave are _____

_____

_____

_____

_____

_____

_____

_____

_____

_____

_____

_____

_____

_____

_____

Outwardly, you are hardly noticeable, little child of mine, but inwardly you are a part of me in every way.

(PHOTO OF MOTHER
DURING SECOND THREE MONTHS)

I visited the doctor/medical caregiver on _____

_____

and heard your heart beating for the first time.
It made me think and feel _____

_____

_____

_____

_____

_____

_____

_____

_____

_____

_____

_____

I had a sonogram on _____

_____

I saw your tiny body in mine. I watched you
move. It made me eager for the day when I would
first hold you in my arms.

(GLUE OR STORE SONOGRAM HERE)

Comments about sonogram: _____

_____

_____

_____

_____

_____

_____

_____

_____

_____

_____

_____

_____

_____

_____

_____

_____

_____

_____

_____

_____

_____

I first wore maternity clothes when I was
_____ months pregnant. Wearing them
for the first time made me feel _____

_____

_____

_____

_____

_____

_____

_____

_____

My favorite maternity clothes are _____

_____

_____

_____

_____

_____

_____

_____

_____

Some interesting comments from family members and friends: _____

The physical changes that I've noticed during the
second three months are _____

_____

_____

_____

_____

_____

_____

_____

_____

_____

_____

_____

_____

_____

_____

_____

_____

_____

_____

_____

My biggest concerns are _____

_____
_____
_____
_____
_____
_____
_____
_____
_____
_____
_____
_____
_____
_____
_____
_____
_____
_____
_____
_____
_____
_____

My biggest concerns are _____

Dreams I have while pregnant include _____

_____

_____

_____

_____

_____

_____

_____

_____

_____

_____

_____

_____

_____

_____

_____

_____

_____

_____

_____

_____

_____

My exercise routine consists of _____

_____

_____

_____

_____

_____

_____

_____

_____

_____

_____

_____

_____

_____

_____

_____

_____

_____

_____

_____

The most important local, national, and world events during my pregnancy have been _____

_____

_____

_____

_____

_____

_____

_____

_____

_____

_____

_____

_____

_____

_____

_____

_____

_____

_____

_____

Popular songs, books, movies, and television shows are _____

_____

_____

_____

_____

_____

_____

_____

_____

_____

_____

_____

_____

_____

_____

_____

_____

_____

_____

_____

First and middle names I would like to give you:

If you are a boy, I like the names _____

_____

_____

_____

_____

_____

_____

_____

If you are a girl, I like the names _____

_____

_____

_____

_____

_____

_____

_____

_____

Some of the suggestions and advice I've received about names are _____

_____

_____

_____

_____

_____

_____

_____

_____

_____

_____

_____

_____

_____

_____

_____

_____

_____

_____

_____

_____

Some people have had funny ways of guessing whether you were a boy or a girl, for example:

_____

_____

_____

_____

_____

_____

_____

_____

_____

_____

_____

_____

_____

_____

_____

_____

_____

_____

_____

_____

_____

Some people have had funny ways of guessing whether you were a boy or a girl, for example:

_____

_____

_____

_____

_____

_____

_____

_____

_____

_____

_____

_____

_____

_____

_____

_____

_____

_____

_____

_____

_____

_____

When others found out that I was pregnant, I
received lots of free advice, such as _____

_____

_____

_____

_____

_____

_____

_____

_____

_____

_____

_____

_____

_____

_____

_____

_____

_____

_____

_____

_____

When others found out that I was pregnant, I
received lots of free advice, such as _____

_____

_____

_____

_____

_____

_____

_____

_____

_____

_____

_____

_____

_____

_____

_____

_____

_____

_____

_____

_____

The first time I felt you move inside me, I _____

_____

_____

_____

_____

_____

_____

It felt like _____

_____

_____

_____

_____

You seem to move the most often when _____

_____

_____

_____

_____

_____

The Last Three Months

You've become much more than a funny feeling now. You weigh about two pounds, and I'm growing bigger as you grow bigger. Here's a picture of "us."

(PHOTO)

Prenatal classes will prepare me to help you enter the world. My labor coach will be _____

_____

I chose this person because _____

_____

_____

_____

_____

Some of the classes we took together included

_____

_____

_____

_____

_____

Special moments we've shared _____

_____

_____

_____

_____

_____

My greatest fears are _____

_____
_____
_____
_____
_____
_____
_____
_____
_____

My greatest expectations are _____

_____
_____
_____
_____
_____
_____
_____
_____
_____
_____
_____

Some of the books I've read to prepare for your arrival

Title	Author	Comments

Some of the books I've read to prepare
for your arrival

Title	Author	Comments

I've begun to go to my medical appointments every two weeks. My doctor/medical caregiver says _____

_____

_____

_____

_____

_____

_____

_____

_____

_____

_____

_____

_____

_____

_____

_____

_____

_____

_____

_____

The most memorable parts of my pregnancy so far have been _____

_____

_____

_____

_____

_____

_____

_____

_____

_____

_____

_____

_____

_____

_____

_____

_____

_____

_____

_____

As the day of your arrival grows nearer, I am
excited about _____

_____

_____

_____

_____

_____

_____

_____

_____

_____

_____

_____

_____

_____

_____

_____

_____

_____

_____

_____

_____

In preparation for your arrival, I decorated your room: _____

_____

_____

_____

_____

_____

_____

_____

_____

_____

_____

_____

_____

_____

_____

_____

_____

_____

_____

_____

Some other things I've done and bought to get
ready for you are _____

_____

_____

_____

_____

_____

_____

_____

_____

_____

_____

_____

_____

_____

_____

_____

_____

_____

_____

Here's a description of baby showers you and I
have been given: _____

_____

_____

_____

_____

_____

_____

_____

_____

_____

_____

_____

_____

_____

_____

_____

_____

_____

_____

_____

Here's a description of baby showers you and I have been given: _____

Here's a description of baby showers you and I
have been given: _____

_____

_____

_____

_____

_____

_____

_____

_____

_____

_____

_____

_____

_____

_____

_____

_____

_____

_____

_____

_____

Here are some of the gifts you and I received:

Gift   Given By

_____

_____

_____

_____

_____

_____

_____

_____

_____

_____

_____

_____

_____

_____

_____

_____

_____

Here are some of the gifts you and I received:

Gift	Given By

I chose Dr. _____
to be your pediatrician.
The _____ _____ office
was located at _____
The reason I chose Dr. _____
is _____

_____

_____

_____

_____

_____

_____

_____

_____

_____

_____

_____

_____

_____

_____

_____

It's hard to believe that almost nine months have passed so quickly. This pregnancy has given me some very important memories: _____

_____

_____

_____

_____

_____

_____

_____

_____

_____

_____

_____

_____

_____

_____

_____

_____

_____

_____

It's hard to believe that almost nine months have passed so quickly. This pregnancy has given me some very important memories: _____

_____

_____

_____

_____

_____

_____

_____

_____

_____

_____

_____

_____

_____

_____

_____

_____

_____

_____

_____

As I look back, this pregnancy has been _____

_____

_____

_____

_____

_____

_____

_____

_____

_____

_____

_____

_____

_____

_____

_____

_____

_____

_____

_____

_____

_____

_____

As I look back, this pregnancy has been _____

_____

_____

_____

_____

_____

_____

_____

_____

_____

_____

_____

_____

_____

_____

_____

_____

_____

_____

_____

_____

The hardest things about being pregnant have been

The hardest things about being pregnant have
been _____

The best things about being pregnant have been

The best things about being pregnant have been

_____

_____

_____

_____

_____

_____

_____

_____

_____

_____

_____

_____

_____

_____

_____

_____

_____

_____

_____

_____

_____

_____

The funniest things about being pregnant have been _____

_____

_____

_____

_____

_____

_____

_____

_____

_____

_____

_____

_____

_____

_____

_____

_____

_____

_____

_____

The funniest things about being pregnant have
been _____

_____

_____

_____

_____

_____

_____

_____

_____

_____

_____

_____

_____

_____

_____

_____

_____

_____

_____

At this point, my sweet little one, you have made
a big difference in my life...and in my body.
I gained

_____ pounds by the end of the seventh month.
_____ pounds by the end of the eighth month.
_____ pounds by the end of the ninth month.

The foods I crave are _____

_____

_____

_____

_____

_____

_____

_____

_____

_____

_____

_____

(PHOTO OF MOTHER
DURING LAST THREE MONTHS)

Of course I've thought about what your birth will be like for me. Some of the things I expect are

_____

_____

_____

_____

_____

_____

_____

_____

_____

_____

_____

_____

_____

_____

_____

_____

_____

_____

_____

_____

Of course I've thought about what your birth will be like for me. Some of the things I expect are

_____

_____

_____

_____

_____

_____

_____

_____

_____

_____

_____

_____

_____

_____

_____

_____

_____

_____

_____

_____

When I packed my suitcase, preparing for your delivery, here's what I took for me:

_____

_____

_____

_____

Here's what I took for you:

_____

_____

_____

_____

Here's a description of the special outfit you came home in:

_____

_____

_____

_____

_____

The Big Event

Finally! You decided to make your appearance!
My contractions began _____
which was _____ compared to my "due date"
estimate. I entered the hospital on _____
_____ at _____.
My labor lasted _____.

You were born at _____ on _____
_____.
You weighed _____ and
were _____ inches long. You had
_____ hair and _____ eyes.

Here are my thoughts about your birth: _____

_____
_____
_____
_____
_____
_____
_____
_____
_____
_____
_____
_____
_____
_____
_____
_____
_____
_____
_____
_____
_____

The first time I saw you, I _____

_____

_____

_____

_____

_____

_____

_____

_____

_____

_____

_____

_____

_____

_____

_____

_____

_____

_____

_____

_____

_____

_____

_____

You were named _____

This name was chosen because _____

_____

_____

_____

_____

_____

_____

_____

_____

_____

_____

_____

_____

_____

_____

_____

_____

You were in the hospital for _____ days.
When I brought you home, I arranged for _____
_____ to help me.
Some of the ways my life and daily routine
changed after you came home included: _____

_____
_____
_____
_____
_____
_____
_____
_____
_____
_____
_____
_____
_____
_____
_____

The following friends and relatives came to visit me while I was in the hospital: _____

_____

_____

_____

_____

_____

_____

_____

_____

_____

_____

_____

_____

_____

_____

_____

_____

_____

_____

_____

_____

_____

Here's a list of family members and friends I notified of your birth: _____

_____

_____

_____

_____

_____

_____

_____

_____

_____

_____

_____

_____

_____

_____

_____

_____

_____

_____

_____

You reminded me of the true meaning of love at first sight. You made me feel like the luckiest mom in the world!

(BABY'S FIRST PHOTO)

I couldn't wait to tell people about you. Some of
the people I called and their reactions were _____

I couldn't wait to tell people about you. Some of the people I called and their reactions were _____

_____

_____

_____

_____

_____

_____

_____

_____

_____

_____

_____

_____

_____

_____

_____

_____

_____

_____

I couldn't wait to tell people about you. Some of the people I called and their reactions were _____

Some of the special people who encouraged and supported me through my months of pregnancy were _____

_____

_____

_____

_____

_____

_____

_____

_____

_____

_____

_____

_____

_____

_____

_____

_____

_____

_____

Here are the names of the family members and friends I sent birth announcements to: _____

Here are the names of the family members and friends I sent birth announcements to: _____

Other Thoughts and Memories: _____

_____
_____
_____
_____
_____
_____
_____
_____
_____
_____
_____
_____
_____
_____
_____
_____
_____
_____
_____
_____
_____
_____
_____
_____

Other Thoughts and Memories: _____

_____
_____
_____
_____
_____
_____
_____
_____
_____
_____
_____
_____
_____
_____
_____
_____
_____
_____
_____
_____
_____
_____

Other Thoughts and Memories: _____

_____

_____

_____

_____

_____

_____

_____

_____

_____

_____

_____

_____

_____

_____

_____

_____

_____

_____

_____

_____

_____

_____

*There's nothing like
a baby's smile
To make your life
feel so worthwhile.*